*the ROUTER**

*REVISED EDITION

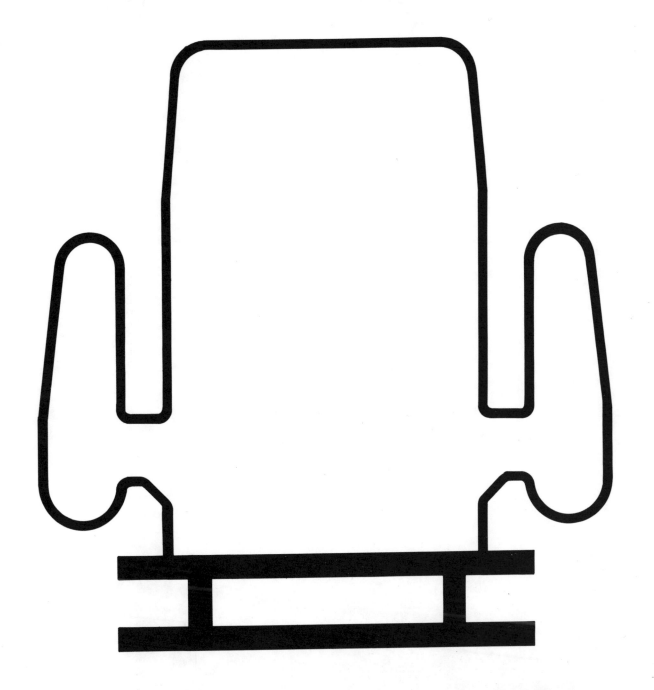

Robert R. Rosendahl

THE ROUTER

* REVISED EDITION

Robert R. Rosendahl

B.Sc.Ed., MA.Ind.Ed., Certified Carpenter

OAK PARK ENTERPRISES LTD.

First Printing 1982
Second Printing 1984
Revised Edition 1986

Canadian Cataloguing in Publication Data

Rosendahl, Robert R.
  The router, revised edition

ISBN 0–919823–02–5

1. Routers (Tools). I. Title.
TT186.R68   621.9'12   C83–00122–2

Printed and Bound in Canada by Friesen Printers
OAK PARK ENTERPRISES LTD.
Box 13, Station A
Winnipeg, Manitoba
R3K 1Z9

Preface

The router is a versatile tool for an unlimited number of applications. There is a need of information on techniques and uses of routers. Basically the router is considered a wood working tool but it can be adapted to practically any material processing, with plastics, laminates, and non ferrous metals.

As his students and workshop participants can attest, Bob has much to teach in the use and care of routers. He claims he is still developing new uses for a most amazing tool, the router.

This revised edition up–dates the original book with additional information on most of the topics as well as many new sections on topics not contained in the first edition. Many colour photos have been included.

Most of the photos were taken in Bob's own shop. In the interest of clarity, safeguards were sometimes removed from the machines. For safe operation of any power tool use safeguards and instructions supplied by the manufacturer of the tool.

Due to possible variances in the quality and condition of machines, materials, and workmanship, the author and the publisher cannot assume responsibility for proper application of techniques or the proper and safe functioning of manufacturered products or reader built projects resulting from directions given in this publication.

Acknowledgements

Thank you to the following for their patience and expertise in providing the photographs and illustrations:

Photographs: Jeff G. Dyck and Dean Rosendahl.

Technical Drawings: D. Bruce Eagleson and John Sellors.

Parrot Drawings: Glenn K. Rosendahl.

Thank you to my students who have been a source of inspiration through their problems and project ideas. Thank you to my workshop and seminar participants who spark new ideas for router applications through their questions and ideas.

Special thanks to James McMillan, Dave Watson, Ed Starsiak, and Rick Rosendahl for sharing their expertise in technical aspects.

Tender words of appreciation to my wife, Reta, for her patience, support, and special talent in organizing and putting together this book.

Contents

Introduction

There is nothing like the thrill of creating your own unique wood products. Modern high speed routers are designed to give special effects to enhance all your wood projects.

The type of wood processing currently being done with routers is similar to the hand carving and molding work accomplished by early wood craftsmen. Hand carving tools and molding planes were early forms of the modern router.

The design of the modern router was delayed until metal processing was advanced to the level where cutters could be developed to withstand the heat and pressure of high speed operation. The high speed of router cutters ensures a smooth finish with or against the wood grain.

It has only been in the last few years that mass production techniques have reduced the price of cutters so they are economically available to carpenters, construction personnel, and craft enthusiasts.

Today, the router is one of the most versatile tools available to the material processor. The flexibility in the type of material processing which can be accomplished with this tool is limited only by the creativeness and skill of the operator.

This book contains the basic instructions and unique ideas that you need to utilize the router more effectively. It is based on my own personal experience – over thirty-five years in the carpentry trade and industrial education.

As you begin to use this tool and discover its versatility and convenience, you will create jigs and products of your own design, as I have.

Unit 1
Router Specifications

What kind of router should I buy? I am constantly being asked this question by prospective router users. This is a very difficult question because for a hundred different people, there could be a hundred different answers. The question produces more questions:

a) Are you a beginner or an experienced woodworker?

b) What type of operations will you expect to perform?

c) What quantity of processing do you expect to do?

d) What kind of cutters/bits will you be using?

e) Are you primarily interested in free hand or table routing?

f) What types of materials do you expect to process?

g) Will you be using the router in situations where you will require accessories? If so, what accessories would be required?

To make a wise decision when purchasing a router, compare the available routers by considering physical features, versatility, accessories, and size/speed. Keep your answers to the above questions in mind as you do this comparing.

Physical Features

Balance

Balance is very important. High speed routers have tremendous torque. Without good balance, the tool can be difficult to control. Handle location can affect the balance. (See figure 1–1). Are the handles off–centre? Are the handles on the base or the motor?

Figure 1–1 To check for balance and handling comfort you must actually hold the router in your hands.

What is the size and shape of the handles? The router should be comfortable for the operator to handle. Before purchasing a router, the buyer should hold it to check for weight, balance, and hand comfort. Some routers have the handles attached to the base. Each time the motor is elevated above the base, the centre of gravity is raised, which changes the balance. This makes the machine top heavy. Compare this to the models with the handles on the motor. Any adjustment, up or down, does not affect the balance or handling.

The total height of the router can affect the balance. Often routers with built–in vacuum systems are top heavy. Built–in vacuum systems are attached to the top of the machine with a pick up on the side and a collection bag to the back. This not only adds to the top heaviness of the machine, but may also affect the side balance.

Single handle routers have very poor balance. This machine is for experienced craftsmen ONLY. It allows one hand operation, which I never recommend. Most accidents with a router (normally few occur) happen when the operator has one hand on the router and the other hand holding the work piece. This is not a safe practise.

Cutter Visability

Routers are available with either an open or closed throat on the base. (See Figure 1-2). The open throat design allows the operator to clearly view the cutter. It is difficult to know where and what the cutter is doing if the operator is unable to see it.

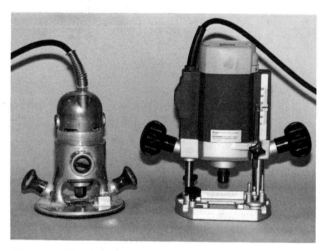

Figure 1-2 Routers have an open or closed throat.

An enclosed throat makes it more difficult for chips and cuttings to be cleared away. Routers with built in vacuum systems can be bad for chip clearance. If the vacuum is unable to pick up the quantity of chips being cut, the cuttings clog the closed throat. (See figure 1-3). This obscures the work and causes cutter interference and inefficiency. For safety, it is necessary to unplug the router and clean out the chips.

Figure 1-3 Closed throat clogged with cuttings.

Base

Routers are available with either a square or round base, or a combination base which is partial round with two straight sides. (See figure 1-4). Straight sides in the router base facilitate the alignment of the work to the bit. In many round bases the bit is not centred to the exteriors of the base. This makes it difficult to line up the work with the bit.

Figure 1-4 Compare the shapes of router base plates.

Some bases allow the bit into tight corners. Sometimes a modification is necessary. (See figure 1-5). If the size or shape of the base is important to a specific operation, this may be an important consideration.

Figure 1-5 This round base plate has been modified for tight corner operation.

Figure 1-7 The router should have a detachable base plate and some system of mounting template guides.

Fence mounting in the base is left or right mounted. Is it easy to mount the fence? This mounting is usually done with screws from the bottom or top thumb screws. The top mounting is maybe more accessible to the operator and therefore more convenient. (See figure 1-6).

Does the router have a detachable base plate? Does the base plate lend itself to mounting template guides? (See figure 1-7). One of the most versatile features about a router is its ability to do template guide cutting. If the router will not hold a guide, the operations possible with the machine are very limited. How does the guide fasten into the base? This is usually a two piece plate with screws. Is there a variety of template sizes available, both in diameter and length? (See figure 1-8). Will it hold inserts for patch cutting?

Figure 1-8 Template guides come in a variety of sizes.

With most routers, the template guides are not interchangeable from router to router. It is possible to fabricate or buy guides for special operations.

A special universally drilled Phenolic base plate with specially fitted solid brass guides is available commercially to fit most makes and models of router. (See figure 1-9).

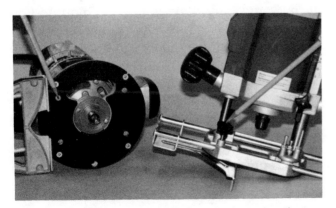

Figure 1-6 The fence is fastened from the bottom or the top.

5

Figure 1–9 Phenolic base plates and solid brass template guides.

For template work, the plunge style router out performs all others. It can be held over the prospective cut with the base flat on the work and the bit above the base. The machine is turned on and then the bit is plunged into the cut at the precise point the operator chooses. (See figure 1–10). Standard routers must be tipped into the work after the machine has been started. (See figure 1–11). Care must be taken to avoid damage to the pattern when tipping the bit into the work.

A special plunge base is now available that makes a plunge router out of a standard model by simply replacing the router base plate. (See figure 1–12).

Figure 1–10 With the plunge style router, the base is held flat on the workpiece while the bit is plunged into the stock.

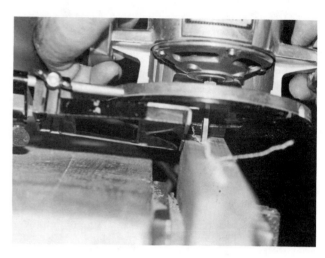

Figure 1–11 With a standard router, the base is held at an angle until the bit can be tipped into the stock.

Figure 1–12 Use a plunge base on a standard router.

Cooling System

All routers have some system of cooling the motor. This is usually accomplished with a bladed fan installed at either end of the armature. Some routers have this fan mounted on the top. This emits a flow of discharged air into the operator's face. Some routers have the fan mounted downward on the chuck end. This allows the expended air to blow down onto the work piece which keeps it clear and free of cuttings. The operator is able to see his/her work better. In case of template cutting, this system keeps the cuttings from jambing between the cutter and the template guide.

Built–In Light

Light is very important for accuracy and for safety. To be of any value, a built–in light should be directed from the top down onto the work piece. If it only comes on when the machine is started, it is useless prior to starting the cut. This is a crucial time for safety and accuracy. Make sure the work area is well lit. Do not depend solely on a built–in router light.

Switch Accessibility

Is the on/off switch in a convenient location? The operator should be able to switch the machine on or off easily without losing control of the machine. Some routers with toggle type switches on the top rim require the operator to release one handle in order to operate the switch. This is not a safe practise. Some toggle type switches do not clearly identify the 'on'and 'off' positions, making it possible to unknowingly plug the machine in with the motor switch in the 'on' position.

Sometimes a spring–loaded switch is built into the right handle. This was primarily designed as a safety feature. However, it is possible to unintentionally start the router when the operator squeezes the handle to pick up the machine. The built–in spring loaded switch in the handle sometimes limits the use of the router, particularily in the under table mounted position.

The most convenient and safe switch is clearly marked and facing the operator. A machine mounted switch that is accessible to the operator while he/she maintains a firm grip on both handles is ideal. (See figure 1–13).

Arbor Locking System

Some routers have a built in arbor lock requiring one wrench to tighten in the bit. (See figure 1–14).

Other routers require two wrenches, one to hold the arbor while the other works the collet system. (See figure 1–15). Both types effectively lock the bit in place.

Figure 1–13 The on/off switch should be easy to use without removing your hands from the handles.

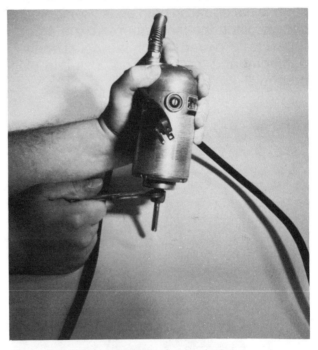

Figure 1–14 This is a one wrench arbor lock.

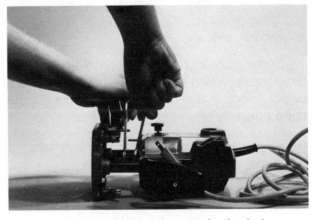

Figure 1–15 This router has a two wrench arbor lock.

Collet size can vary from one quarter inch, three eighths inch, to one half inch. These are the cutter shank sizes. When using diameters other than these standard sizes, be sure to use the proper adaptors provided by approved manufacturers. Always use the bit with the largest shank size that will fit the collet on the router. The larger the shank, the less shank vibration there will be and the smoother the cutter will run.

Basically all router chucks function the same. They all use a collet system to lock in the bit. A router chuck that will receive one quarter, three eighths, and one half inch shanks are always the best buy because these are the standard sizes.

Some chucks have a split collet that is tapered on both ends. (See figure 1–16). The taper is not equal on both ends. Remember to always place the long taper into the arbor. If this rule is disregarded, the collet may be damaged and the bit will not lock into place properly.

Figure 1–17 This collet is fixed. The collet and the bit lift out when the nut is unscrewed.

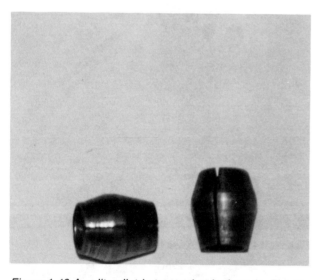

Figure 1–16 A split collet is tapered at both ends. The long taper fits into the arbor.

Some chucks have a fixed collet, which is a real asset when extracting a bit. As the nut is unscrewed, it lifts the collet and the bit out. (See figure 1–17).

Most machines that offer one quarter, three eighths, and one half inch collets have separate single tapered collets. These function better than the bushing type. (See figure 1–18).

Figure 1–18 Single taper collets function better than the bushing type.

Some routers offer replaceable chucks. (See figure 1–19). This is a good feature. Most wear and damage that occurs to a router usually involves the chuck because of the constant mounting and dismounting of bits. If the chuck is a part of the armature shaft, damaged threads could mean an expensive repair. (See figure 1–20). A replacement chuck is relatively inexpensive in comparison.

Figure 1–19 This router has a replaceable chuck.

Figure 1–20 The chuck on this machine is attached permanently to the armature shaft.

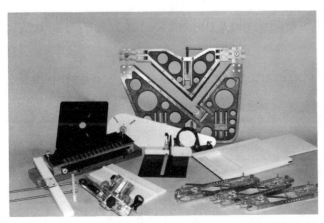

Figure 1–21 Manufactured accessories are available for use with the router.

Versatility

Specialized routers are necessary for highly specialized operations, such as, sign printing or veneer trimming. Some of these operations may require a reverse rotation router.

Some routers lend themselves to simpler adaptation for either over or under operation.

There is a wide variety of accessories available, which may suit one router more readily than another.

Accessories And Jigs

There are many manufactured accessories and jigs available. (See figure 1–21). These include the radial arm saw adapter, the power plane, the hinge jig, the laminate trimmer guide, the dovetail jig, the mortising base plate, template guides, stair template, parallel guide fence, trammel points, spacer fences, circle jigs, and pattern jigs. Some of these are discussed in later units.

Most jigs and accessories are readily adjustable to work with any make of router. However, it may be wise to match accessories and jigs with the router if you know before hand what jigs, template guides, etc. you will need.

In addition to manufactured jigs, there are unlimited individually designed and built jigs and accessories. This is where individual creativity comes in. During the years that I have used a router I have designed hundreds of different jigs, each to suit a current product design and purpose. Some of these are discussed in the jig and product section.

Size and Speed

The horse power rating of the motor can vary from one–eighth HP to five HP and many industrial routers have ten HP motors.

Consider the size and bulk as well as the horse power, when comparing the size of routers. Routers are available with speeds from 16,000 to 35,000 RPM capacity. If the job is heavy, like routing stairs or thick cut–off work, a heavy machine will give stability and will eliminate excessive vibration. Light cutting and delicate moldings are better done with a light weight, high speed machine. Physical size and weight are important for ease of operation.

SUMMARY

Choose a router because of its balance; handling comfort; base shape, size, and detachability; open throat; template and accessory fittings; downdraft cooling fan; convenient switch on the motor; and power/size to suit the operation intended. Do not choose a router for its built in vacuum system, built in light, or computer features. These items are of dubious value.

I own numerous routers of all makes and sizes. This makes it easier to evaluate the individual capabilities of each router. Also, it is beneficial to have a number of routers if only for the convenience of not having to change bits and attachments for each different cut.

Not every one can nor wants to have many routers. A basic first router for general purpose use should be of medium size, with seven eighths to one and one half horse power. It should be capable of receiving a bit shank larger than the standard one quarter inch. The router is the most inexpensive part of a routing operation.

The plunge style router is a tremendous improvement over the standard type. I am still finding new operations for the plunge router that would be impossible with the standard machine. For versatility and safety, try a plunge router or buy a plunge base to attach to your standard router which will give you the plunge feature without investing in a new router.

"If you can't try it, don't buy it!"

Choose high quality carbide tipped bits to use with the router. The initial cost for these bits seems high; but, nothing is saved by purchasing inexpensive bits that never cut properly and lose their temper after the second cut.

Some bits get priority because of their multitude of uses. The following should be part of a basic collection of first router bits. If cost is a factor purchase one at a time as funds become available.

Basic Collection of Router Bits (carbide tipped)

1 — ¼'' or ⅜'' Straight bit (two flute).

1 — ⅜'' Radius rounding over bit with interchangeable ball bearing pilot — may use the same bit for beading.

1 — ¼'' Radius Roman Ogee (With ball bearing pilot).

1 — ¼'' Panel cutting bit.

1 — ⅜'' Flush trim bit (with ball bearing pilot).

1 — ⅜'' Rabbeting bit (with interchangeable bearings to allow the bit to cut ¼'', ⅜'', and ½'' width of the rabbet).

1 — ½'' Dovetail bit.

A good router and the first bit on this list will get you started. Add to the collection as the need arises.

Safety is a major consideration with any power equipment. Routers are no exception. Always follow manufacturer's directions for safe operation of power tools. Use this step by step checklist to evaluate and rate your safe work habits when using the router:

1. Keep the work area clean.

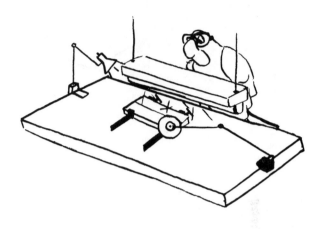

3. Work in a well–lit area.
4. Be sure the motor is properly grounded.

2. Power tools should not be exposed to rain or used in damp or wet environments.

5. Wear eye protection and the proper apparel. Loose clothing, jewelry, and long hair may get caught in moving parts. Safety glasses are a must.

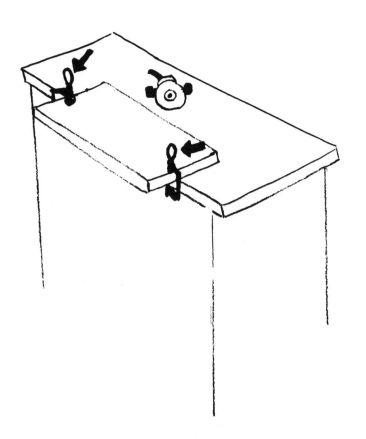

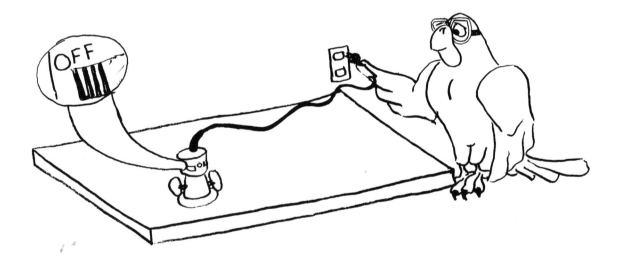

6. With clamps or a vise, fasten the work piece securely in a table stand.

7. Be sure the bit or cutter is securely locked in the chuck. Check the base to be sure it is tightly fastened to the motor.

8. Unplug the router from its power source before changing bits or making adjustments.

9. Before plugging in the cord be sure the motor switch is at the 'OFF' position.

10. Never start or stop the router under full cutting load.

11. Hold the router base firmly on the work with the bit clear of the wood before turning on the switch. A firm grip is necessary to over–come starting torque.

12. Keep fingers and hands away from revolving bits and cutters.

13. With both hands on the handles, turn the switch to 'ON' and feed smoothly in the correct direction without forcing the tool.

14. Use only bits, grinders, or cutters that are manufactured especially for the router. The high speed and torque of the router could throw or disintegrate attachments meant for a slower RPM drill or other tool.

15. When the cut is complete, turn the motor switch to 'OFF' without lifting the router from the work.

16. Be sure the router bit has stopped before laying the router down.

17. Never touch the bit or cutter immediately after use because it is hot.

18. Do not use power tools and accessories in work beyond their capabilities.

19. Never use a router or other electric tool in the vicinity of flammables which may cause combustion or explosion.

20. Clean, sharp tools give the best and safest performance.

21. Use a safety guide pin in the hole provided when you do free hand molding with a table mounted router. (If no safety pin hole is provided be sure to drill one in a suitable location).

"A MACHINE WORTH USING IS WORTH TAKING CARE OF."

Unit 3
Use Of The Router

Because of its versatility the router should be a first choice in portable power tools.

It is used to cut desired thicknesses or depths into or through wood or other materials. Cut intricate joints, such as, the dovetail. Use it to shape or round edges. Cut gains, dados, grooves, mortises, and irregular shapes with the router. Using the router with jigs and accessories adds to its versatility. (See figure 3–1). Material processing that can be done with a router is basically unlimited.

Router operation involves a step by step procedure that does not vary greatly from one project to the next.

Disconnect the plug from the power source.

Mount the desired bit. Set the depth of cut.

Secure the stock, guides, templates etc.

With the motor switch at 'OFF' plug into the power source.

Turn the motor switch to 'ON'.

Make the cut.

Turn the motor switch to 'OFF' and disconnect the power plug.

Dismount the bit.

Figure 3–1 Router jigs and accessories.

Mounting and Dismounting Bits

Be sure the router is UNPLUGGED from the power source and the motor switch is in the 'OFF' position before inserting or removing cutters and bits. A faulty switch can cause the machine to start without being turned on if there is a source of power.

Router bits are mounted in a collet type chuck. This may be a one piece collet or a two piece split collet assembly. (See figure 3–2).

Figure 3–2 A two piece split collet and one piece collets.

With separate sleeves, most routers can be used with one eighth, one quarter, three eighths, and one half inch shank size cutters. Always choose the largest shank size bit that will fit the collet. (See figure 3–3). This will cut down on vibration and heat build–up.

Figure 3–3 Three 1/2'' bits with different size shanks.

Before inserting the bit, make sure the shank and collet are clean and free of nicks. The bit should fit snugly. Insert the shank of the bit to within one eighth inch of bottoming out.

During use all cutters generate a tremendous amount of heat. This space helps prevent the heat buildup from transferring to the router armature. The armature could be damaged by excessive heat.

Before tightening the collet, check to see that the split in the sleeve is in line with the split in the collet. Then securely tighten the collet nut on the chuck to mount the bit. Router chucks have either a wrench/arbor lock system or a two wrench system for tightening in the bit. (See figure 3–4 and 3–5).

Figure 3–4 Wrench/arbor locking system.

Figure 3–5 Two wrench locking system.

CAUTION: Loose cutters and bits not only will damage the collet; but, they will almost always spiral through and ruin the work piece.

To dismount the bit from the collet chuck, reverse the mounting procedure.

CAUTION: To loosen a bit that is stuck, tap lightly near the shank end with a soft block of wood. Never use a hammer, wrench, or plier to loosen the bit.

Depth of Cut

With the desired bit locked in place, the operator is ready to adjust and set the depth of cut.

CAUTION: The router is unplugged and the motor switch is in the 'OFF' position.

There are two common types of depth adjustment. They are the ring type and the stopper pole and scale type.

Ring Type

With the router base positioned flat on the work piece, adjust the cutting bit until its tip contacts the work piece. Clamp the motor in this position with the base lock. Loosen the depth ring and adjust the ring upwards from the base to the desired depth of cut. This depth may be measured or gauged by using the actual inset or hinge intended for the operation. (See figure 3–6). Hold the depth ring firmly in place, while you loosen the lock nut on the base to allow the motor to slide down to the depth ring. Tighten the base nut.

CAUTION: On these routers, the motor may be removed after loosening the base lock. During adjustment, be sure to hold the motor, as it could accidentally slide through the base and fall to the floor.

Figure 3–6 Set the ring type depth adjustment with the hinge to be used on the project.

Stopper Pole and Scale

The depth adjustment on a plunge router is the stopper pole and scale type.

With the router base positioned flat on the work piece, loosen the plunge lock lever and lower the cutter to contact the work piece. Lock the plunge lever and the scale nut. From the reading on the scale, raise the stopper pole to the desired depth of cut and lock it in place. This depth may be measured or gauged by using the actual inset or hinge intended for the operation. (See figure 3–7).

After loosening the plunge lock, plunge the router bit until the stopper pole comes into contact with the stopper block. This gives the proper depth of cut. This type of depth adjust-ment also has depth setting screws, that allow the cut to be done in stages. This setting adjustment is ideal for deep mortise cuts.

Figure 3–7 Set the depth of cut on the stopper pole and scale type adjustment.

Secure The Stock

Each project must be held securely, either squeezed in a wood vise or clamped to a work bench. ***Never attempt to hold the work piece with one hand while routing with the other.***

Clamp or secure the stock in such a way that the securing devices do not interfere with or obstruct the cutting lines you intend to make.

Ready To Start The Cut

With the motor switch in the 'OFF' position plug the router cord into the power outlet. To overcome the effects of starting torque, be sure to have a firm grip on the router handles before engaging the 'ON' switch.

Direction Of Feed

As with any power tool, the direction the machine is passed across the material is very important. The cutter or bit should always rotate into the material. (See figure 3–8).

When molding a decorative edge in the outside of a piece of stock, always do the end grain side first, moving the router from left to right. Then move along the straight grain edge. Do the other end grain side and finish up with the other straight grain side. (See figure 3–9).

When molding the edge of an inside circle, move the router clockwise. (See figure 3–10). In all cases these rules prevent the cutter from climbing away from the work piece.

When working with a particularly snarly, cross grain piece of stock, it is wise to score along the entire edge before making the dec-orative cut. (See figure 3–11). The final cut will clean up the scored edge, prevent splinter-ing, and result in a professional job.

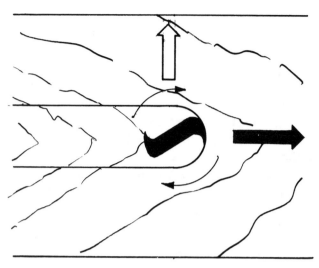

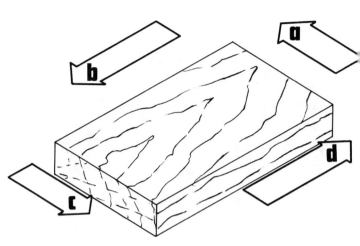

Figure 3–8 The cutter rotates into the stock. The large white and black arrows indicate the direction of push exerted by the cutter. The small curved arrows show the cutter rotation.

Figure 3–9 Mold the outside edge of a piece of stock by a) mold the end grain, left to right, b) do the straight grain side moving left to right, c) finish the other end grain side, and d) do the remaining straight grain edge.

Figure 3–10 The direction of feed is important in router usage. Be sure the cutter is rotating into the stock by moving left to right on outside edges and clockwise on inside cuts.

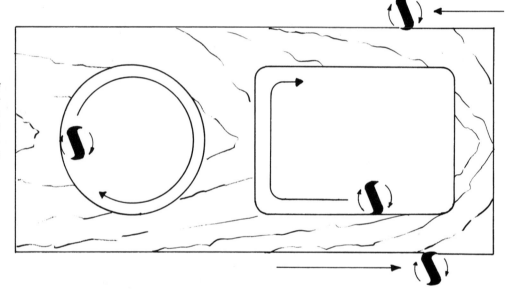

Figure 3–11 Score a snarly piece of stock prior to applying a decorative mold.

22

To run a dado completely around a piece of stock, cut the two end grain dados first, then make the straight grain dados. (See figure 3–12). To prevent splitting out of the end grain, use a scrap piece of wood as a support and back up.

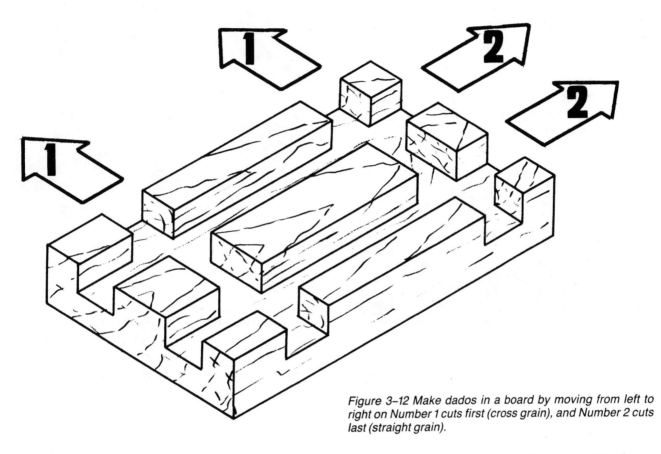

Figure 3–12 Make dados in a board by moving from left to right on Number 1 cuts first (cross grain), and Number 2 cuts last (straight grain).

Speed Of Feed

Always operate the router under full load and move along smoothly.

> CAUTION: Let the router come to top speed before you engage it into the cut. Many carbide tipped bits are damaged because the operator neglected this important step.

The speed of feeding the router over the work piece depends on the size of the cut, size of the cutter, and the hardness of the material being processed. Feeding too fast overloads the motor and produces poor quality work. Feeding too slowly causes the cutter to over heat which results in burn marks on the work piece and possible damage to the cutter. If, for some reason, you must pause in the middle of a cut, move the router bit away from the work piece.

Three important factors to remember in router usage are: keep cutting tools sharp, cut with the wood grain where possible, and do not force the speed of cut.

Through experience, an operator gains a feel for router efficiency. The operator knows instinctively when the machine is working at an efficient feed speed.

New computerized lights on the router, that dim or glow brighter, add little to the efficient operation of the machine.

Standard Or Plunge

There are basically two types of router. The standard style is where the bit protrudes below the base by the depth of cut set by the operator. With a standard router the bit must be held free of the work until the machine reaches top speed. Then it is tipped or pulled into the work piece at the desired point. This procedure takes experience and practice to make smooth accurate cuts. (See figure 3–13). When tipping the router bit in at an angle you are adding extra strain on the cutter and the machine which could damage the bit. Also, the risk of the bit coming in contact with your pattern is greater. Many patterns have been damaged from this type of operation.

Figure 3–14 The plunge router can be held flat on the stock with the bit raised until the motor is at full power. Then the bit is plunged into the cut and locked into place until the cut is completed.

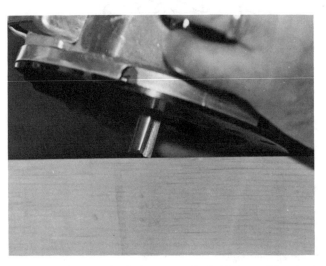

Figure 3–13 A standard router must be held clear of the stock until it has reached full power and then it is tipped into the cut.

On a plunge style router, the bit is above the base until the operator plunges it into the work piece to the depth previously set. Once the bit is in the work, a lever locks it in position. With a plunge style router, the operator can rest the base on the work piece in a flat position. The router is turned on, the bit is plunged into the work at this point, and a lock lever secures it in this position. (See figure 3–14). When the cut is finished, the operator can release the lock lever and return the bit to the above base position. This is a good safety feature because the bit is up out of the way, when it is not in use. Because the base can be held in a flat stable position at all times, the plunge router is especially good for template cutting, free hand designs, and middle of the work cuts.

A plunge base that will fit all routers is now available. If you intend to do much pattern work or procedures that require tipping in the bit, it may be economical to invest in a plunge base for your standard router. (See figure 3–15).

Figure 3–15 Fit a plunge base on your standard router.

Unit 4
Router Bits and Cutters

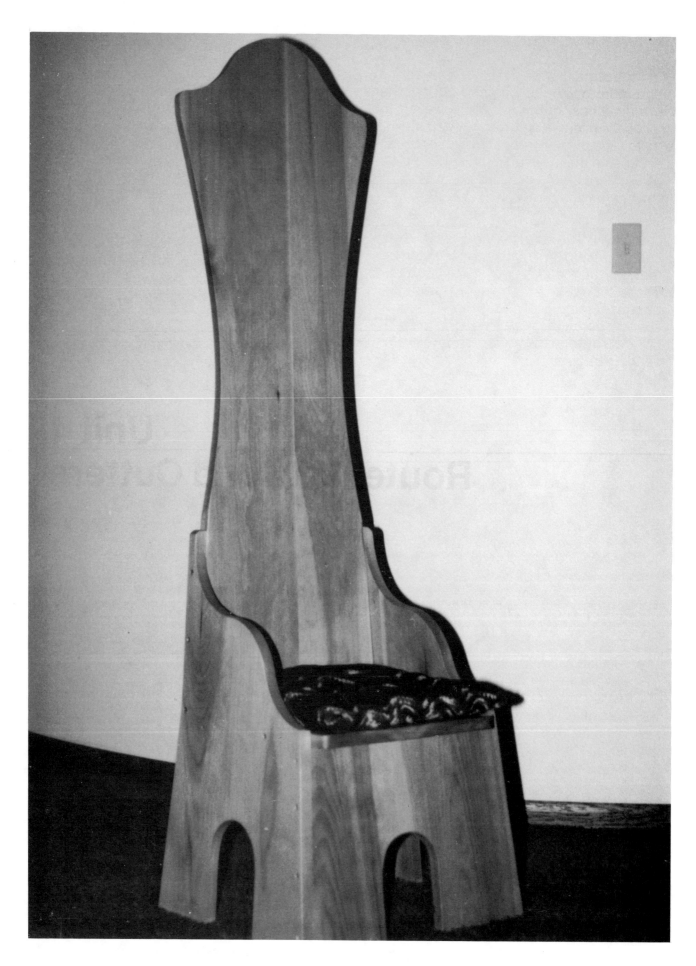

26

It is possible that a router owner may spend more on router bits and cutters than the original cost of the router. However, the most costly mistake a purchaser can make is to try to save by buying poor quality cutters. It is cheaper in the long run to buy only once.

All router cutters and bits are available in both imperial and metric sizes.

> CAUTION: There are several low speed cutters, rasps, and many grinding stones that will fit the collet of most routers. These should **NEVER** be used in a router because they are designed for slow speed operation. When used in a high speed router, they will disintegrate sending fragments of cutter or stone in all directions. This may result in serious injury for the operator and others in the work area.

Use only high quality bits and cutters. The steel in high quality cutters is designed to withstand amazing punishment without shank or bit damage.

Most good quality bits have a high hook angle and wide open gullets for easy chip clearance. The cutting edge is radially relieved to resist rubbing, burning, or picking up the work. These cutters are all individually balanced.

In most cases the operator can expect to get fifteen sharpenings from good quality carbide tipped bits and cutters. See the section on the care of carbide tipped bits and cutters in Unit 9.

High speed steel bits are cheaper to purchase. However, once they are burnt the temper is gone and the bit will no longer hold a cutting edge.

Bits And Cutters

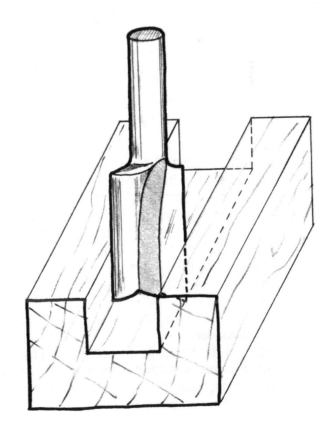

1. Straight Bits
— This is the most versatile of all bits.
— Available in all shank sizes.
— Comes in all sizes both imperial and metric.
— Designed for high speed production.
— Ideal for multiple cutting, mortise cutting, trimming, dadoing, and rabbeting.
— Most straight bits are relieved for normal plunging jobs.
— Comes with single or two flute, stagger tooth and chip breaker.

2. Rounding Over Bit
- — Available in all shank sizes.
- — Available in all radiuses from ¼'' to 1''.
- — Can be purchased with or without a pilot.
- — Used for decorative molding of one quarter rounds.
- — Used for architectural moldings.
- — May be used with or without a fence.

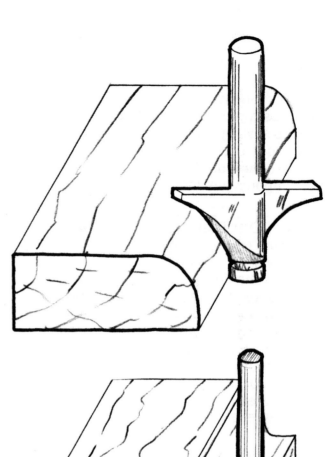

3. Roman Ogee Bit
- — Available in all shank sizes.
- — Comes in radiuses from ⁵⁄₃₂'' to ⅜''.
- — Cuts all materials: solid woods, plywood and composition materials.
- — This is the most popular of all decorative cutters.
- — Used for furniture, cabinets, and industrial projects.
- — Contains a ball bearing pilot.
- — This is a must for woodworkers.
- — A multitude of molds may be produced, depending on set ups and combinations.
- — Will mold small coves and round overs.

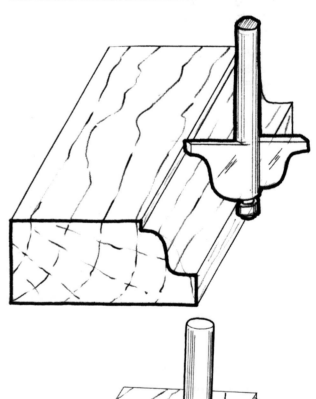

4. Combination Panel Bit
- — Comes with a drill through point which allows for self starting.
- — Available with single or double flute. The double flute operates with less chatter, faster and smoother cut, and less load on the router.
- — May be used with or without a template guide.
- — This bit is a must for the average woodworker.
- — Ideal for the building industry, used for cutting out window openings, door openings, sheathing, and electrical outlet boxes in panelling.

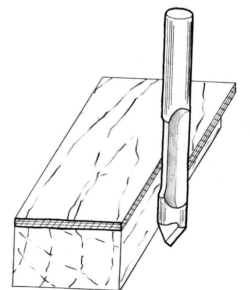

5. Flush Trim Bit
- — Available in all shank sizes.
- — Has ⅜'' to ¾'' cutting diameter.
- — Available with two or three flutes.
- — Used to trim veneers or laminates.
- — Long reach cut available.
- — Economical.
- — ½'' to 2 ½'' cutting depth.

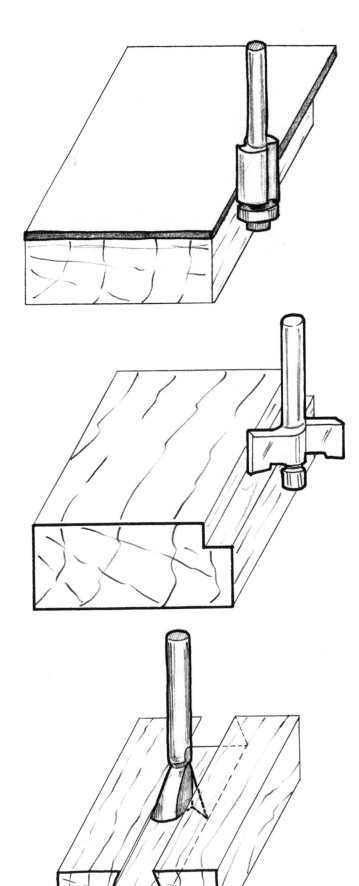

6. Rabbeting Bits
- — Available in all shank sizes.
- — Available in 1'' to 2'' diameter cutting edge
- — two flutes.
- — Available with or without ball bearing pilots.
- — Available in screw–on arbors or fixed arbors.
- — Used for plain or irregular rabbeting.
- — Used for rabbeting cabinet doors, picture insets.
- — Used for step joints or lap joints.
- — This is an ideal bit for cabinet builders.
- — Works excellent on all solid woods and composition materials.
- — The cutter is relieved on top and bottom for chip free routing.
- — Interchangeable pilot bearings to make deep or shallow rabbets.

7. Dovetail Bit
- — Available in all shank sizes.
- — Available with 9 to 14 degree angles.
- — Has high radial and axial angles for clean, smooth cutting.
- — Especially designed to use with dovetail jigs to make drawer finger joints and French dovetailing.
- — Used for joints on fine furniture and high production processes.
- — Works well in all solid woods, composition materials, plywoods, and laminates.

8. Rounding Over Bit With Boring Point
— Available in all shank sizes.
— Available in radiuses from ¼'' to 1''.
— Ideal for plunge cutting.
— Used for decorative molding and multiple cutting.
— Use for architectural moldings.
— Must be used with a fence or template guide.
— Good for circle work, such as picture frames, and table tops.

9. Ogee Bit
— Available in all shank sizes.
— Available with radius sizes from ⁵⁄₃₂'' to ³⁄₈'' which makes diameter cuts of ⁵⁄₈'' to 1¼'.
— Has no pilot.
— Ideal for plunge cutting.
— Used for decorative designs cut into the face of the material.
— Used for cabinet door designs.

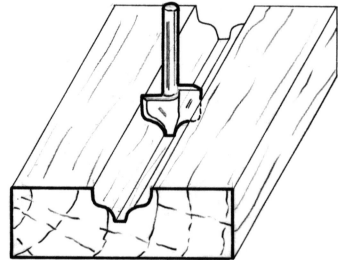

10. Classical Mortising Bit
— Available in all shank sizes.
— Two flutes.
— Special designed for deep mortises.
— Mortises a smooth flat scratch free bottom, with small radius in the corner.
— Cuts a clean rounding over at the top of the mortise, if set at a depth of ⁹⁄₁₆'' to ⁵⁄₈''.
— Ideal for candy & nut dishes, pencil boxes, coasters, or any classical shape where a smooth bottom is required.

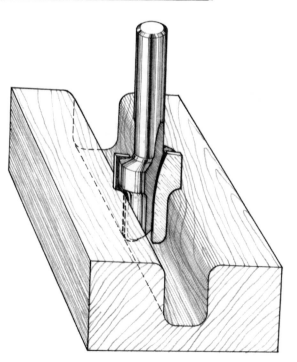

11. Combination Veining & Core Box Bit

— Available in ¼'' shank.
— Solid carbide.
— Two flutes.
— Two bits in one.
— Used for sign writing.
— Used when precise detail is to be accented on furniture, or veining is required.

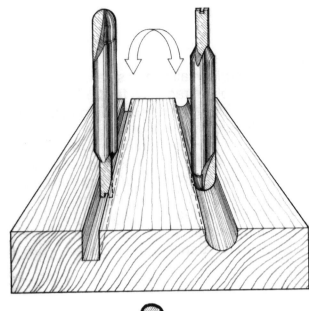

12. Mortising Bits

— Comes in all shank sizes.
— Comes in ½'' to 1½'' cutting diameters.
— Has a 5 degree relief angle to tight face fit.
— Ideal for mortising housed stringer stairs. This is a high production cutting bit.
— Routs a very smooth bottom.

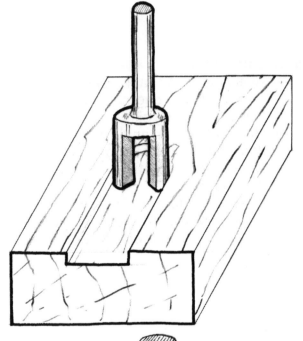

13. Slotting Cutters

— Available in all shank sizes.
— Has Kerf sizes from ¹⁄₁₆'' to ¼'' in ¹⁄₆₄'' increments.
— Comes in two, three, and four wing models.
— These cutters may be stacked on an arbor much like a dado blade.
— This cutter is ideal for slotting T mold-ings.
— Can be used for rabbeting, grooving, and multiple slotting with the use of collars.

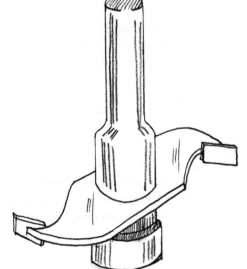

14. Cove Bit
— Available in all shank sizes.
— Available in radiuses from ¼'' to 1''.
— Used for decorative moldings on cabinets and fine furniture.
— Works well on hard and soft solid woods and on composition materials.
— May be used with or without ball bearing pilot.
— The up shear cutting angle clears chips out fast and clean.
— Used for architectural moldings.

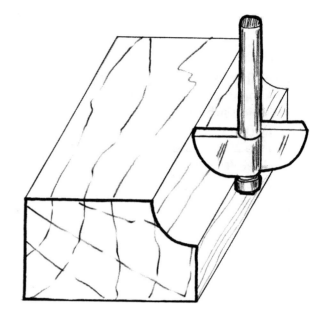

15. Chamfer Bits
— Available in all shank sizes.
— Comes with 45 degree angle.
— Has ball bearing pilot.
— Has high shear angle for fast, clean cuts and chatter free operation.
— Used for decorative, chamfer, and bevel cuts.
— Used for pattern work.
— Works well in hard and soft solid wood, composition materials, and plastic materials.

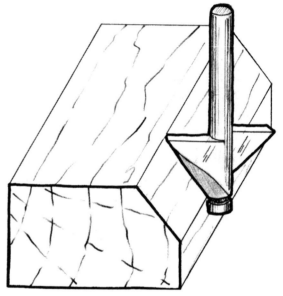

16. Rounding Over Beading Bit With Pilot
— Available in all shank sizes.
— Available in radiuses of ¼'' to 1''.
— Ball bearing pilot guide may be changed to form a beading bit.
— Used for architectural moldings, rounding corners in both side and end grain.
— Cuts well in hard and soft solid wood and for composition materials.
— Has a high axial and radial hook angles to ensure maximum chip removal for a smooth cut.

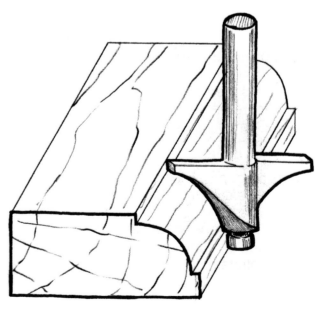

32

17. Round Nose or Core Box Bit

— Comes in width of cut sizes from ⅛'' to 1½''.
— Available in all shank sizes.
— Comes in single or two flute.
— A high up–shear angle lifts the chips clear to give a smooth perfect radius cut.
— Used by furniture builders, pattern shops, and many woodworkers.
— Cuts well in soft and hard woods as well as composition materials.

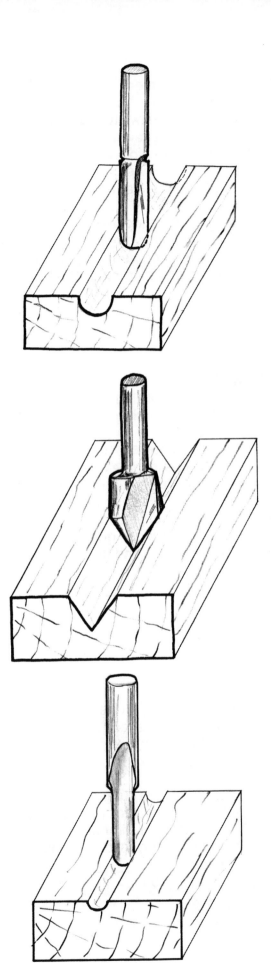

18. V Grooving Bits

— Designed for both shallow and deep grooving.
— Used for veining decorative panelling.
— Excellent for cutting solid woods, composition materials, and vinyl covered materials.
— Used for general decorative cutting.
— Used for planking and v joint.
— Ideal for mitering.

19. Veining Bits

— Available with round or flat bottom.
— Cuts well in solid stock and composition materials.
— Used for straight line for panelling.
— Used for fine free–hand lettering.
— Used for fine inlay work.

20. Laminate Trimmers

— Available in all shank sizes.
— Available with two to four flutes.
— Comes with straight or Helix design.
— Available in solid carbide.
— Available in designs to make flush, 15–25 degree, and over hung trimming.
— Ideal for trimming plastic laminate.
— All trimmers have ball bearing pilots.
— Used for wood veneers, for trimming, splicing, patching, and inlays.

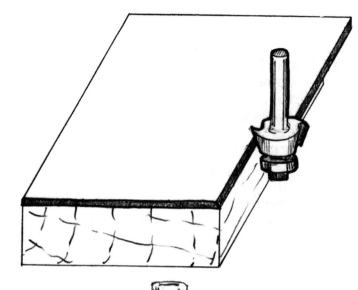

21. Spiral Bits

— Available in all shank sizes.
— Available in cutting diameters of ⅛'' to ½''.
— Spiral cuts both up and down cutting.
— Spiral bits eliminate chip build up.
— Ideal for cutting abrasive materials such as magnesium, aluminum, and a wide variety of plastics.
— These bits are designed for both template and free hand through cutting.

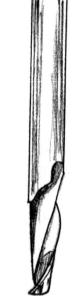

22. Combination Bull Nose Bit

— Available in all shank sizes.
— Available in two flutes.
— Consists of 3 sizes of bullnose (⅛'', ¼'', ⅜'').
— Ideal for pattern cutting.
— Cuts and trims stock in one pass.
— May be used for trimming.
— Used for cutting solid wood, veneer, or plywood.
— Three bits in one.

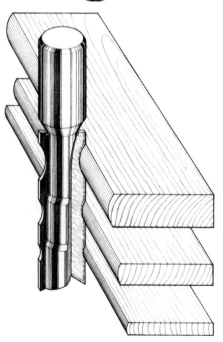

23. Key Slot Bit
— Available in ¼'' shank.
— Designed to plunge cut.
— Carbide tipped.
— Single flute.
— Hole diameter ³⁄₁₆''.
— Under cut diameter ³⁄₈''.
— Used for hole hanging plaques and pictures flush to the wall without the aid of wires or mechanical fasteners.

24. Finger Pull Bit
— Available in all shank sizes.
— Designed to plunge cut.
— Carbide tipped.
— Two flutes.
— Ideal for making finger pulls and han-dles flush or surface mounted.
— Ideal for inside radius routing.

25. Classical Mold Cutter
— Available in all shank sizes.
— Two flutes.
— Carbide tipped.
— Ideal for decorative edging and built up moldings.
— Cuts well in all types of wood materials.
— Comes in three sizes ³⁄₄'', ⁷⁄₈'', 1''.

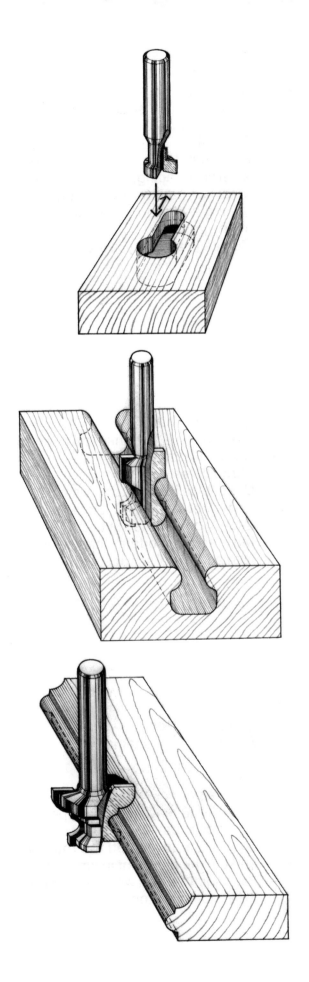

26. Bull Nose Bit
— Available in ½'' shank size.
— Carbide tipped.
— Two flutes.
— Excellent for half round shapes and external beading.
— Ideal for pattern and irregular shape cutting and rounding over both edges in one pass.
— Comes in a variety of sizes.

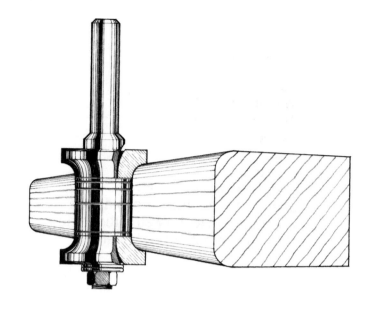

27. Finger Joint Cutter
— Available in ½'' shank size.
— Carbide tipped.
— Three flutes.
— Used to splice end to end stock.
— A perfect match for stock up to ⅞'' thick in one single set up.
— May accommodate thicker material with additional set ups.

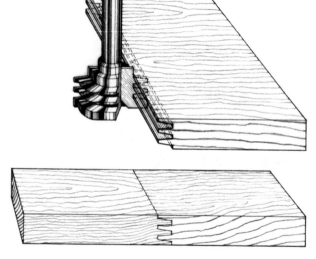

28. Glue Joint Cutter
— Available in ½'' shank.
— Carbide tipped.
— Two flutes.
— Make a perfect fit.
— Ideal for joining narrow strips to glue up for door panels.
— May be set to joint off the rough edge and cut the glue joint in one operation.
— Ideal joint to use when splicing stock for a wide table top.

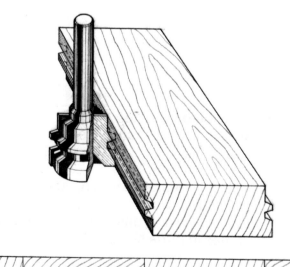

36

29. Fiberglass Bit
— Comes in all shank sizes.
— Available in cutting diameters of ⅛" to ⅜".
— The milling on the bit is a diamond design.
— This is a specialty cutter used for cutting phenolic, epoxy glass, and non-metallic abrasive materials.
— It is available with or without the drill point which is useful for plunge cutting.

30. Blank Cutter
— Available in all shank sizes.
— Available in ½" to 2 ½" cutting diameters.
— May be ground to any shape.
— Blank knives and shanks are available.
— Used to match hand made moldings.
— Used to make unlimited types of molds.

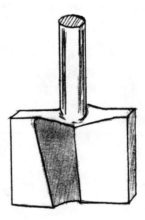

38

Unit 5
Table Mounting

A. Router Tables

The router is a versatile machine when used as a portable unit. However, it becomes even more versatile when mounted in a table. The router may be mounted under, over, on-the-side, or on-an-angle. For line production it is possible to have many routers mounted on the same table to facilitate step by step production without constant set ups and changes. For long run production of a special mold, use two or more routers mounted on the same table. Each router has a bit mounted to do a part of the mold. As the stock is passed by the routers, the mold is cut in steps, until it emerges from the last router in the desired shape.

An under the table mounted router is capable of performing many of the same operations as a shaper. There are many router tables on the market. Most of them are made of sheet metal or light aluminum. I have found these very unsatisfactory because of the tremendous vibration encountered. A light weight, flimsy table can even be dangerous. Being unable to find a suitable manufactured router table, I decided to make my own. The design and construction of a router

Figure 5–A–1 This old router table is still in use.

table might be a good first project, because it is necessary for so many operations.

I built my first router table over thirty years ago. I am still using it. (See figure 5–A–1). By necessity, it was built on a job site a long way from the shop. We had run out of quarter round and cove moldings. To make the necessary moldings, I fashioned the above router table from scrap. It did the job. The laminate top was added when we returned to the shop. An effective router table should be simple and sturdy.

When making a router table, some important considerations are: size of the table top, height of the table, storage, vibration free construction, and a convenient method of mounting the router in the table top.

After many years of using a router for unlimited applications, I found it most useful mounted in a table. However, I was always upset at the tedious task of fastening the router under the table top. If the top was thick and strong, I lost height for extending the cutters. If the top was thin, it would be weak and vibrate. The other tedious task was to change cutters on the table mounted router when it was bolted to the top. This involved reaching underneath in the dark with various wrenches to mount and dismount the bits and cutters.

I experimented with many types of material before I found the phenolic material which I now use for router base plates. I first tried 1/4'' aluminum, but I found the surface gave off a black oxide onto the stock being molded. It also had a tendency to vibrate. I then tried plexiglass. This was great until it began spaulding out around the mounting screws. I finally bought an eleven inch square piece of phenolic board 1/4'' thick. This was the answer. I have used phenolic base plates ever since.

The phenolic plate replaces the normal router base plate. A hole is cut in the ¾'' plywood table top (this can have a plastic laminate covering). A ⅜'' by ¼'' rabbet cut all around the hole allows the phenolic base plate to fit snugly in place and flush with the table top. (See figure 5–A–2). No further fastening is required. Be sure the base plate fits tightly in the table hole. The weight of the router will hold it in place. Any adjustment, bit/cutter mounting or dismounting, can now be done by lifting the router and base plate out of the rabbeted hole and up on the table top. (See figure 5–A–3).

Adjustments are made at a comfortable working level. The router and base plate are then set back in the rabbet in the table top. Phenolic base plates can be purchased to fit most makes and models of router. (See figure 5–A–4).

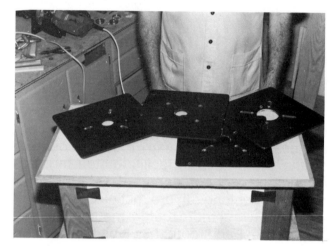

Figure 5–A–4 Eleven inch phenolic base plates are drilled to fit most router makes.

Figure 5–A–2 The 11'' phenolic base plate fits on the table rabbet.

Once the router is table mounted, it may be compared to a shaper. We should be aware of some safety considerations. Sometimes we tend to forget with free hand routing and try to use the pilot on the bit as a guide. When we approach the cutter with a piece of stock, the stock comes in contact with the cutter before it can reach the pilot. This is when we need to use the SAFETY GUIDE PIN. (See figure 5–A–5). When the safety pin or fulcrum is in place, it is possible to guide the work piece into the cutter while resting it firmly against the pin. (See figure 5–A–6).

Figure 5–A–3 The router and plate are pulled up in a table top position at a comfortable working level for bit adjustments.

Figure 5–A–5 Always use a safety guide pin for molding irregular shaped stock.

42

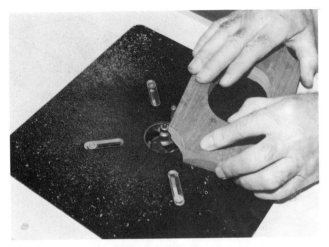

Figure 5-A-6 The safety guide pin helps to hold the stock as it approaches the cutter.

The brass insert is used to narrow the bit hole in the base plate. (See figure 5-A-7). In this position it gives added support to small stock.

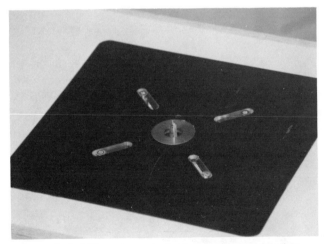

Figure 5-A-7 Use a brass insert to narrow the bit hole.

B. Router Table Fences
Table Fence

When using a router table as a shaper, one important accessory is a fence. Sometimes a shop made device is far superior to anything available on the market. A router table fence must be securely fastened to the table with either clamps or other fastening devices. It is not necessary for the fence to be parallel or lined up with the table or anything. Regardless of the angle of attachment to the table, it is always lined up to the router cutter. (See figure 5-B-1).

Figure 5-B-1 The table fence is always lined up to the bit.

When constructing a router table fence use a strong knot free piece of stock. It should be about two inches wide by one inch thick and slightly longer than the table top width. The fence should have two half holes that are centered. One half hole will be on the under side for chip clearance. The other half hole will be in the face side of the fence to allow space for pilot bits to run freely. All four edges of the fence should be slightly chamfered. This will prevent the build up of cuttings between the work piece and the fence. (See figure 5-B-2). Check the fence from time to time to be sure that it is straight. It may need dressing occasionally to maintain the straightness.

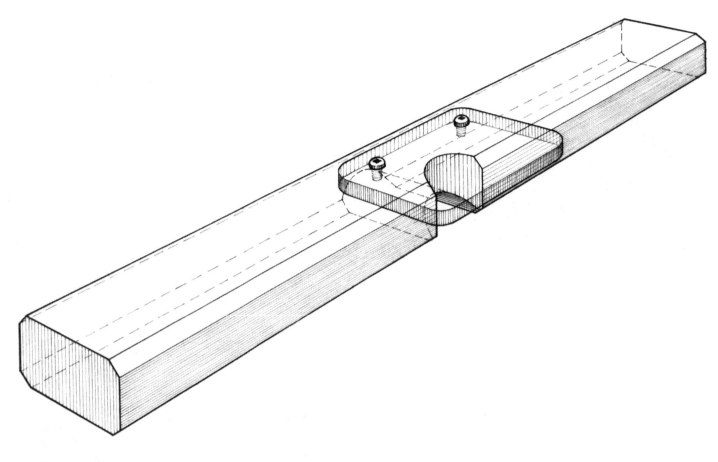

Figure 5–B–2 A table fence should have two half holes, chamfered edges, and a guard.

When using a decorative bit such as a Roman ogee, sometimes the chipping and long tear out may be prevented by selecting a new fence, clamping one end to the table top, and swinging the fence into position while the bit is running. The bit will cut an exact pattern in the leading edge of the fence, which acts as a chip breaker when the work piece is cut. Be sure to fasten the fence securely before cutting stock and use a fence guard whenever possible. (See figure 5–B–3). You may like to keep a stock of table fences on hand to use in the above manner.

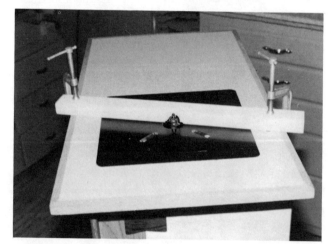

Figure 5–B–3 When an exact bit pattern is cut into the leading edge of the table fence, it acts as a chip breaker.

NOTE: Do not trap the stock between the fence and the cutter. (See figures 5–B–4 and 5–B–5).

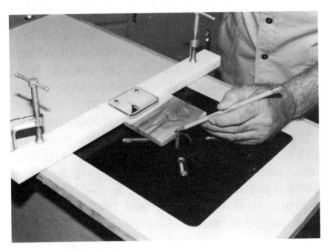

Figure 5–B–4 WRONG WAY. The fence is positioned wrong in this illustration. The stock will become trapped between the fence and the bit.

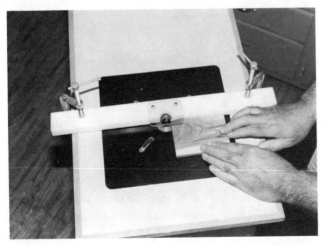

Figure 5–B–5 RIGHT WAY. The fence is positioned to enable the bit to mold the edge of the stock without trapping it.

CAUTION: Always use ''C'' clamps to fasten the fence to the router table. The quick adjusting clamps have a tendency to vibrate loose thus allowing the fence to move away. (See figure 5–B–6).

Figure 5–B–6 The fence should be secured with C clamps (a), rather than quick adjusting clamps (b).

Jointer Fence

When it is necessary to joint stock on a table mounted router, use a stepped fence. (See figure 5–B–7). It is important that the amount of material being removed equals the step distance in the fence. It is convenient to have several of these step fences with different depths, for jointing short pieces of stock. This is a very accurate method. Just a straight two flute cutter is sufficient for this operation.

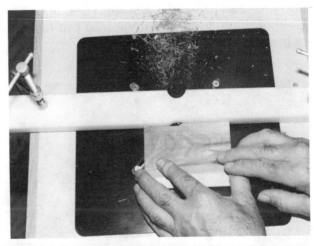

Figure 5–B–7 Joint small peices of stock on the table mounted router by using a stepped fence.

However, if you are jointing very short pieces of stock, use a very small diameter bit. The clearance hole in the fence needs to be only slightly larger than the bits. When jointing end grained stock, be sure to start one end in for a short distance. Then turn the stock over and joint from the other edge of the same end. This will prevent tear out at the finish of the cut. (See figure 5-B-8). Use a guard on all table fences.

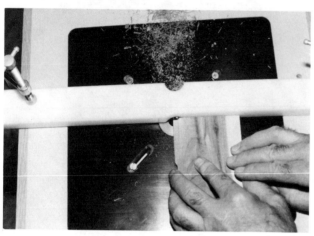

Figure 5-B-8 To joint end grain, start the stock in for a short distance. Then turn the stock over and joint from the other edge of the same end.

Curved Fence
Occasionally, the need arises to mold the edges of a curved or circular work piece. It is convenient to cut a curved fence to match the work piece design, clamp this fence in place, and proceed to mold the stock. (See figure 5-B-9). Always feed the stock into the rotation of the cutter.

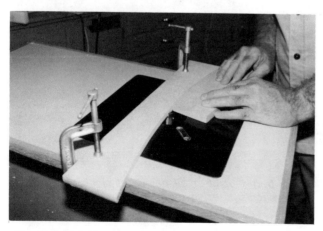

Figure 5-B-9 Use a curved fence to match the work piece when molding curved stock.

C. Hold Downs And Push Sticks
Hold downs and push sticks are a must if you intend to make moldings on the table router. The best method is to take a wide board and mold the edge into a quarter round cove or a decorative mold. Then cut the molding off and mold the edge of the remaining board. Repeat this procedure until all the moldings are made. However, you may find that it is more economical to make moldings from rippings. If this is the case some hold downs and push sticks will be necessary. The hold down should be band sawed from clear ash because of its bending qualities. This may be clamped to exert pressure down on the work piece both at the in feed and the out feed together with a feather board to exert inward pressure. (See figure 5-C-1). This will ensure that the stock will be held firmly against the fence.

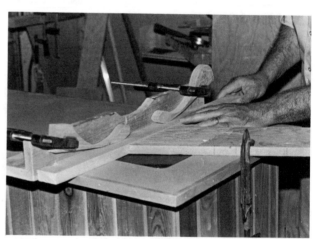

Figure 5-C-1 A shop made hold down can be used to hold the stock down at the infeed and the outfeed while a feather board holds the stock against the fence.

Some type of push stick should be used for safety. Push sticks should be designed to suit the task. Some may be designed with a flat surface and an end hook to act as a hold down and to feed the work piece forward. (See figure 5-C-2). The angled push stick gives hand clearance at the fence. (See figure 5-C-3). Other push sticks may have a groove to hold the work piece down and against the fence with an end hook for forward push. (See figure 5-C-4).

Figure 5-C-2 A simple push stick creates downward and forward push on the stock.

Figure 5-C-3 An angled push stick allows hand clearance at the fence while exerting downward and forward push on the stock.

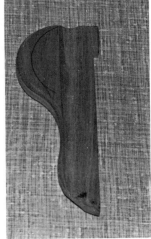

Figure 5-C-4 This grooved push stick provides inward as well as downward and forward push on the stock.

Whichever method or design you choose, remember, the finished mold will always be smooth and perfect if it is not allowed to vibrate while it passes the cutter. For safety, always use a push stick with narrow or hard to manage stock. Be sure the part of the push stick that receives hand contact is sliver free and has a smooth easy-grip design. A simple push block is a square piece of wood with a shaker peg handle. (See figure 5-C-5).

Figure 5-C-5 For a simple push block use a square of wood with a shaker peg handle.

When the edges of the square get cut up, remove the shaker peg and replace the push block with a new piece.

D. Novelty Box

Novelty boxes are decorative, useful, and interesting. Small wooden boxes are used to store jewelry, coins, pins, and a multitude of other small items. They can be made of exotic wood such as zebra wood or padouk. Make these boxes of cedar, oak, or any wood you like to work with. The wooden boxes can be finished in clear to take advantage of decorative wood grain. They can be painted or designed to dress up a plain wood. Novelty wooden boxes make interesting gifts. Put a musical movement in a gift box.

Basically a wooden box is very easy to make. A box is made up of six pieces; two sides, two ends, a top, and a bottom. The easiest way to make a box is to glue the six pieces into a block and then cut it apart to make a lid and a bottom. (See figure 5-D-1).

Cut the box pieces to the desired size.

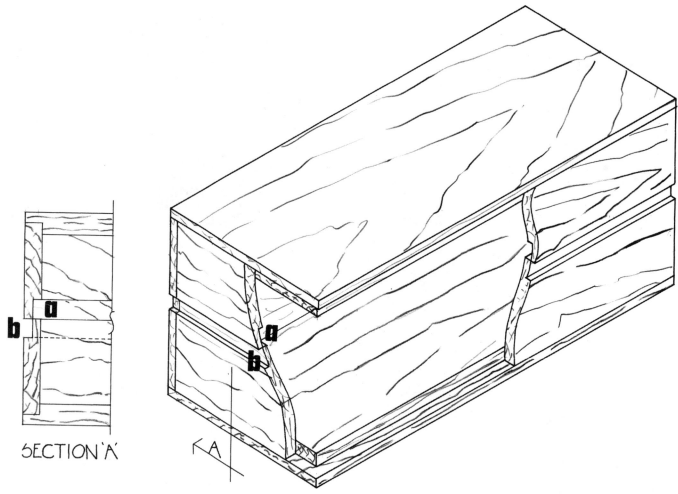

SECTION 'A'

Figure 5-D-1 Novelty box design.

Rabbet all around the top and bottom pieces. This rabbet must be the width to match the stock thickness and half the depth of the material being used.

Rabbet only the ends of each side. When cutting end grain, use a backup piece to prevent splintering. (See figure 5-D-2).

To make the lid/bottom division, run a dado groove near the top on the inside of each end and each side. (See figure 5-D-3). Make certain all the dados line up on the inside when the pieces are glued together. (See figure 5-D-4).

Figure 5-D-2 When cross grain cuts are made, always use a backer piece to prevent splintering.

Figure 5-D-3 Run a dado on the inside of the sides and ends of the box pieces where you wish the lid/bottom division to be.

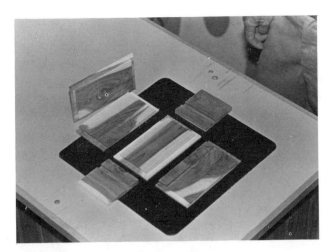

Figure 5-D-4 The lid dados must line up.

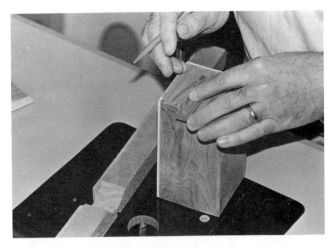

Figure 5-D-6 Mark the outside dados.

NOTE: Mark the top and bottom on the outside of the box before gluing. Also mark the position of the inside dados.

Glue the box together. (See figure 5-D-5). During the cut apart operation, the top of the box will go against the fence. Lightly mark the location for the outside dado on the outside of the box. This dado must be below the inside dado by a spacing of slightly less than the bit width. (See figure 5-D-6). Set the fence to cut this dado. Using the same bit you used for the inside dado, cut the outside dados in the two box sides first. (See figure 5-D-7).

Figure 5-D-7 Cut the outside dados only in the box ends.

NOTE: Be sure that the bit is cutting deep enough to meet the inside dado. These cuts should free the lid from the bottom, when all the outside dados are completed. (See figure 5-D-8).

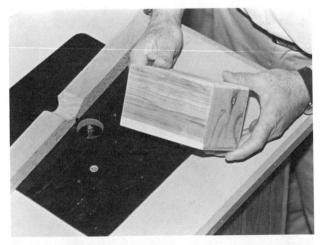

Figure 5-D-5 Mark the top of the box and the position of the inside dados. Then glue the box pieces together.

Figure 5-D-8 Check to be sure that the outside dado is meeting the inside dado.

Tape a filler piece the exact width and depth of the dado into the two side grooves. (See figure 5-D-9). The reason for these filler pieces is to prevent the box from collapsing into the bit when the remaining end dados are cut. Cut the end dados. Now, the box should have an outside dado cut all the way around. (See figure 5-D-10). Remove the filler pieces from the side grooves. The top should be separate from the bottom. (See figure 5-D-11).

Figure 5-D-10 Cut outside dados in the sides of the box.

Figure 5-D-11 The box lid and bottom are separated.

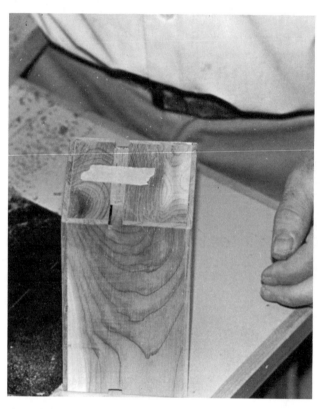

Figure 5-D-9 Tape filler pieces in the end dados.

The inside and outside dados now become rabbets allowing the inside rabbet to lap over the outside rabbet. This makes the lid fit perfectly. (See figure 5-D-12).

Sand the box lightly. Finish the novelty box as desired.

Figure 5-D-12 The inside and outside dados are now rabbets which create a perfect fitting lid.

NOTE: When rabbeting, try to avoid using straight bits. Use a rabbeting bit instead. (See rabbeting bit in Unit 4). If you must use a straight bit remember to *ONLY* rabbet no greater than one half the bit width at one pass. (See figure 5–D–13). If greater than one half the bit is used, the bit is pushing the material away rather than cutting it. This leaves a rough and ragged edge. (See figure 5–D–14).

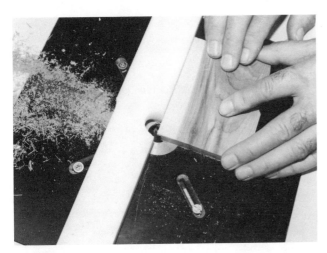

Figure 5–D–13 With a straight bit make a rabbet no greater than half the bit width in one pass.

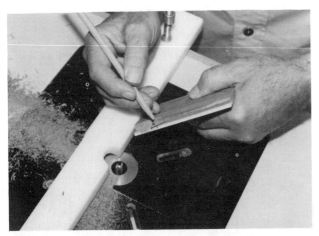

Figure 5–D–14 When more than half the straight bit is used for a rabbet it leaves a ragged edge.

E. Moldings

Produce moldings with your table mounted router. The router is an ideal machine to use in production of a simple mold or an exotic compound mold.

Most times molds can be accomplished with a minimum of bits. The profile of each cutter may not be the only shape that it can produce. A plain rounding over bit can also be used as a beading bit by simply changing the ball bearing pilot. Better still, take the pilot off and use the bit with a fence. This will allow adjustment in the cutter and also the amount of profile that the fence allows to be exposed.

Quite often someone will show up at one of my router seminars with a short piece of molding and this question, "Where can I purchase a bit to cut this mold?"

In most cases the mold had not been done with one bit. It probably took two or more bits and a number of setups with maybe a different mold on the edge of several strips. Often these strips stack into one larger molding. The variety of compound molds that can be made with a few basic bits and your router is only limited by your imagination.

The following figures illustrate setups for a few basic molds and several built–up molds that require a number of bits and operations. (See figures 5–E–1 to 5–E–17).

Figure 5–E–1 Stopped and through fluting. Use a core box bit.

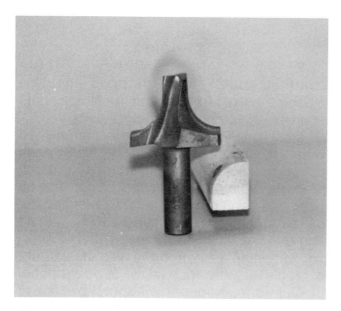

Figure 5–E–2 Quarter round. Plunge rounding over bit.

Figure 5–E–5 Corner mold. Roman Ogee bit.

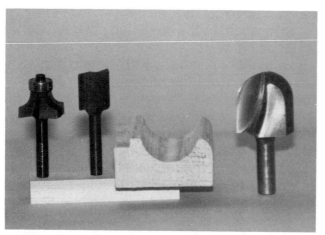

Figure 5–E–3 Chalk rail mold is made with three bits: core box bit, 3/4" two flute straight bit, and rounding over bit.

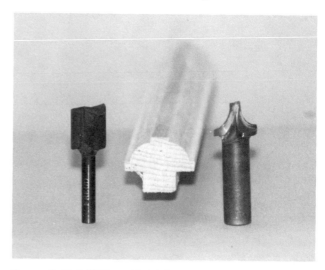

Figure 5–E–6 "T" mold. 3/4" two flute straight bit and a plunge rounding over bit.

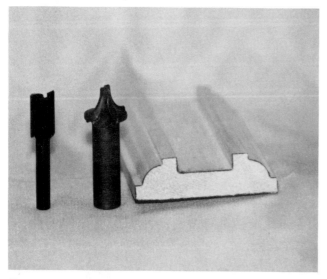

Figure 5–E–4 Bed Mold uses a plunge rounding over bit and a 3/4" two flute straight bit.

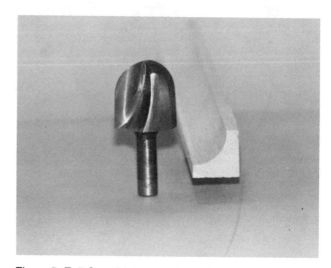

Figure 5–E–7 Cove Mold. Core box bit.

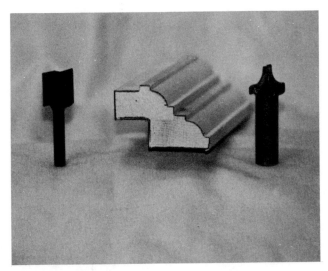

Figure 5-E-8 Stepped crown mold. 3/4" two flute straight bit and a plunge rounding over bit.

Figure 5-E-11 Built-up corner cove molding. Four bits: raised panel door bit, 3/4" two flute straight bit, chamfering bit, and plunge rounding over bit.

Figure 5-E-9 Corner mold. Plunge rounding over bit.

Figure 5-E-12 Panel splice. Beading bit.

Figure 5-E-10 Provincial mold. Plunge rounding over bit.

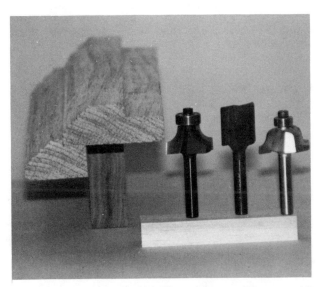

Figure 5-E-13 Crown mold. Three bits: rounding over bit, 3/4" two flute straight bit, and Roman Ogee bit.

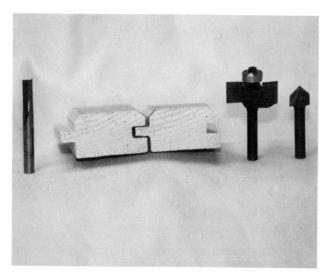

Figure 5–E–14 Tongue and groove V joint. Three bits: "V" groove bit, 1/4" two flute straight bit, and 3/8" rabbeting bit.

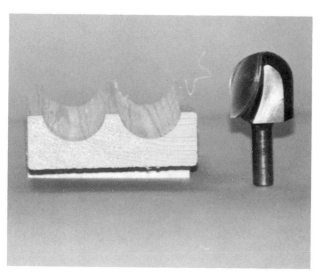

Figure 5–E–16 Fluting (Large). Core box bit.

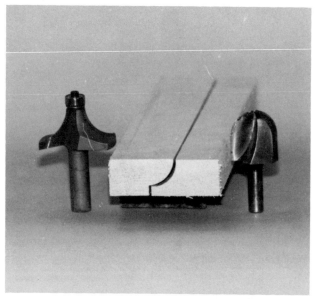

Figure 5–E–15 Drop Leaf Table mold. Rounding over bit and core box bit.

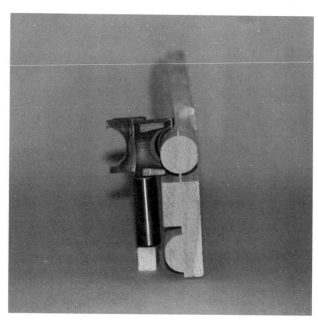

Figure 5–E–17 Beading mold and dowelling. 1/2" round bull nose bit.

Unit 6
Using Jigs, Fixtures, and Accessories

The router can be used for virtually unlimited operations when it is used with jigs, fixtures, and accessories.

This section is devoted to router uses. It includes practical tips and procedures, as well as project ideas.

With various bits and jigs the router can be used to make many creative and novel products.

Design your own jigs and projects. There are millions of ideas not yet discovered or developed.

A. Using The Router Fence

Most router manufacturers provide a versatile fence that can be used for many operations. Some fences have extremely good adjusting mechanisms that allow them to be used for straight and curved work, for external and internal cuts, for centre points in circle cutting, and for jointing with an offset shoe. (See figure 6-A-1).

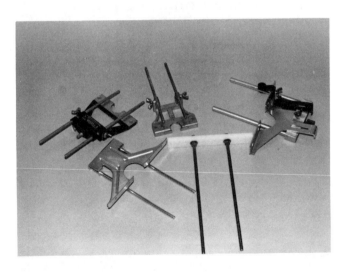

Figure 6-A-1 Manufactured router fences.

A fence may be used to cut dados to receive an adjustable shelf strip. (See figures 6-A-2 and 6-A-3).

Use the fence to make dados to receive decorative inlays. (See figure 6-A-4).

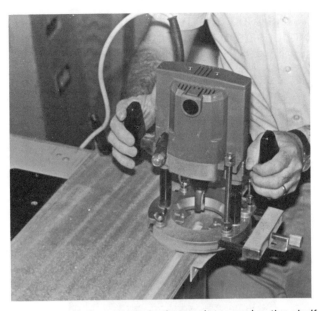

Figure 6-A-2 Cut a dado in the stock to receive the shelf strip.

Figure 6-A-3 Install the adjustable shelf strip in the dado.

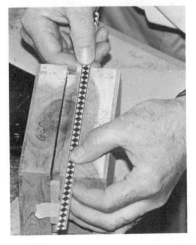

Figure 6-A-4 Decorative inlays can be applied to an edge or surface.

It is important that the fence is used on the proper side of the router. The bit must pull the stock up to the fence rather than push it away. The direction of feed is important. (See figure 6–A–5).

Figure 6–A–5 The fence is mounted on the left side of the router.

The fence is useful when cutting a mortise. (See figure 6–A–6). When using a standard router it may be necessary to modify the fence to make it possible to tip the router bit into the stock. As this takes a bit of practise, start with scrap pieces of lumber.

A plunge style router is ideal for use with a fence because of its versatile positioning, plunging feature.

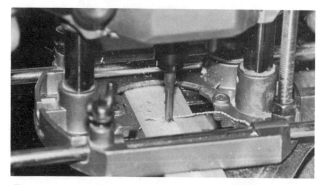

Figure 6–A–6 Making mortises.

To start a mortise cut always mount the fence on the left. Line the router bit over the slot to be cut, start the router, and plunge cut to a preset depth. Always advance from left to right. Plunge style routers are equipped with a step down depth adjusting unit. It is possible to cut an extremely deep mortise by presetting the depth and making three passes. (See figure 6–A–7).

Figure 6–A–7 The step down depth adjustment is useful for making deep mortises.

B. Self Centering Pins

Another handy jig that works well on a router is self centering pins. (See figure 6–B–1). These pins are attached to the base plate of the router. They must be in line with the bit centre and equal distant from the centre. To use you simply place the base plate over the stock to be mortised, twist until each pin comes in contact with an opposite side of the stock, plunge the bit into the material, and cut a mortise which will always be exactly centre in the stock regardless of its width. (See figure 6–B–2).

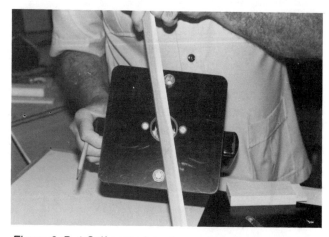

Figure 6–B–1 Self centering pins are attached to the base plate.

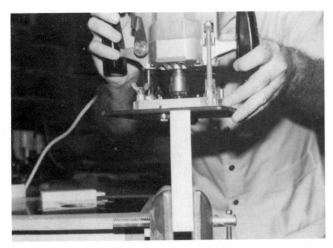

Figure 6–B–2 The self centering pins make it easy to make a centre mortise in any size stock without measuring.

C. Divider Jig

It is often thought that a router can only be used for making fancy edges. Actually the router is an excellent tool for just straight cutting. It is often possible to cut out and mold the product in one simple operation. A simple profile can be time consuming and difficult to cut accurately when many exact replicas are required, as with dividers. (See figure 6–C–1). The router and a jig simplifies and improves the quality of repeat cuttings.

Select the size and shape of divider to be used. Make a simple jig to hold the stock and outline the desired shape. (See figure 6–C–2).

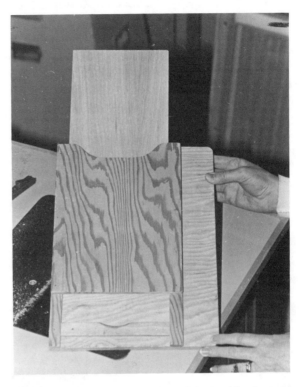

Figure 6–C–2 A divider jig consists of the backing board and a slot to receive the stock.

Figure 6–C–1 Divider storage.

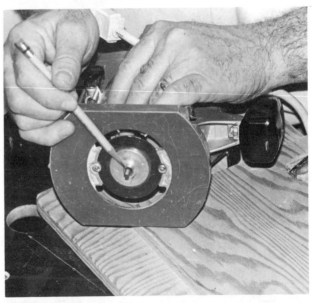

Figure 6–C–3 Use a straight 1/4" bit and a template guide in the router to cut thin plywood dividers.

For thin plywood, which makes an excellent divider, use a straight ¼" bit and a template. (See figure 6–C–3).

Mount the bit and template in the router. Preset the depth of cut to protrude through the stock. A slightly deeper cut helps to leave a smooth edge. Slide the stock into the jig. (See figure 6–C–4). Pass the router across the jig being careful to keep the template guide in constant contact with the pattern. Remove the finished divider. (See figure 6–C–5). Repeat this operation until the desired number of dividers are produced. All the dividers will be exactly the same.

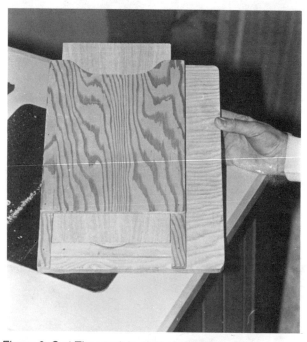

Figure 6–C–4 The stock is slid into the jig as far as it will go.

Figure 6–C–5 Rout along the profile edge of the jig and remove the finished divider.

NOTE: As the finished product will only be as good as the pattern, take time to make an exact pattern.

D. Spacer Fences
Box Joint

The box joint is a very simple way to join two pieces of wood. (See figure 6–D–1). However, to be effective the contact points in the joint must meet exactly. There is not room for even a slight error. For this exact operation, make a box joint with a table mounted router and a spacer fence. The important point with a spacer fence is that the bit, the space, and the fence must all be the same width. Example: When using a ⅜'' bit and a ⅜'' fence, the space between the bit and the fence must be ⅜''. (See figure 6–D–2).

Spacer fences come in standard sizes of ¼'', ⅜'', and ½''. Other sizes may be constructed to suit any size of bit. The fence should protrude slightly less than half the chosen bit size. This provides chip clearance space.

Clamp the spacer fence securely to the router table. Adjust the depth of cut to the same height as the material thickness being cut. When you cut box joints, the pieces must be offset by the the diameter of the bit being used to ensure that the pieces will be flush when assembled. Place a backer piece of scrap material behind the work pieces to eliminate chipping. Clamp these three trial pieces together. (See figure 6–D–3). With the extended edge tight against the fence make the first cut. (See figure 6–D–4). Slip the first cut over the fence and pass the pieces through again to make the second cut. Place the second cut over the fence to make the third cut and so on until the entire end has been slotted. (See figure 6–D–5).

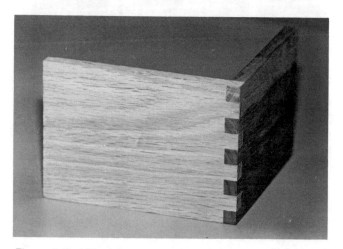

Figure 6–D–1 Box joint.

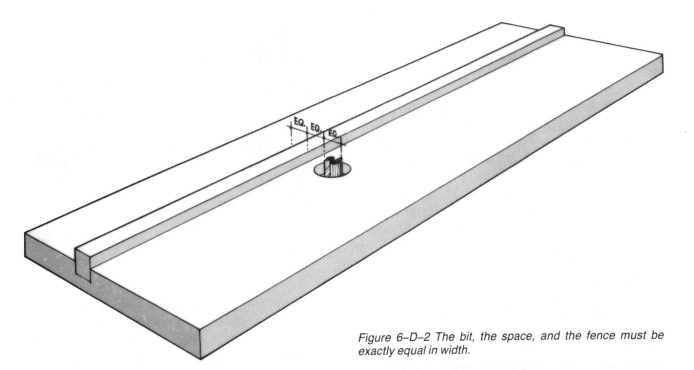

Figure 6–D–2 The bit, the space, and the fence must be exactly equal in width.

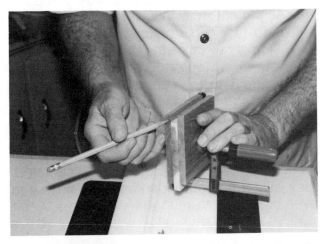

Figure 6–D–3 Off set and clamp the box pieces together with a backer piece.

Figure 6–D–5 Place each cut over the fence to make the next cut until the entire end is slotted.

Figure 6–D–4 Make the first cut.

Figure 6–D–6 Use a back–up block behind to hold the pieces square.

NOTE: If you are unsure of being able to hold these pieces square with the fence while passing them across the bit, use a square back–up block behind. (See figure 6–D–6).

This repeat method ensures that all the cuts will interlock perfectly. Unclamp the pieces and assemble the box joint. (See figure 6-D-7).

NOTE: If the joint is too loose or too tight adjust the fence slightly. To tighten the joint, move the fence away from the bit. To loosen the joint, move the fence towards the bit. This adjustment can easily be done while the jig is clamped in place by tapping in or out with a light hammer (My fine adjusting tool).

Once the sample joint is a desired fit, drill bolt holes through the jig and table top at each end. Bolt the spacer fence in place with 1/4'' flat headed bolts and wing nuts. Remove the clamps. Each time you wish to use this spacer fence just bolt it in place for quick alignment. If you have several other sizes of spacer fence, follow the above procedure with each, always clamping first to establish a perfect fit. Do not drill a multitude of holes in your table top. Once you have the desired fit, drill holes up through the first spacer bolt holes in the table top and through the clamped spacer fence. This way the same two holes in the table top will match all the spacer fences. Bolting the spacer fences eliminates set up time for future use of the fences.

Figure 6-D-7 Test the joint for fit.

Once the sample piece is complete and you have a perfect fit, you can make a simple alignment jig. Select a piece of stock and run a series of dados on the flat side with the wood grain. (See figure 6-D-8).

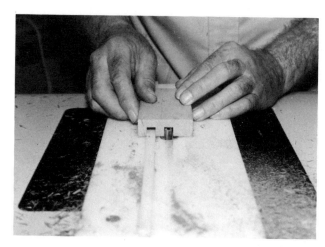

Figure 6-D-8 Make a simple alignment jig.

Example: If you are using a 3/8'' spacer fence, your alignment jig will have a series of dados 3/8'' apart and 3/8'' deep. If you were constructing a small box out of 3/8'' material, you now could place the four side pieces in your alignment jig as follows: side one is in the first dado, side two is on top snug against side one, side three is in the second dado, and side four is on top snug against side three. (See figure 6-D-9). You may glue a back-up block into the third dado. Clamp all four box pieces to the back-up block and holder. Run the box joints into your pieces as shown above. This will give a perfect offset without measuring. When the pieces are assembled, they will form a four sided box with flush and even box joints.

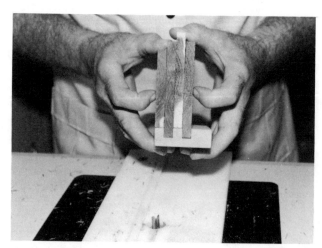

Figure 6-D-9 The alignment jig makes it unnecessary to measure off-sets.

Lattice Pot Mat

Another product easily made with the spacer fence is a simple mat to protect a table top from hot pots. (See figure 6–D–10). Make a hot pot mat by using a flat piece of wood the dimensions you wish the mat to be. The operation is similar to the box joint except the cuts are made in the flat of the wood rather than the ends. The depth of cut must be set at slightly more than half the thickness of the mat material. The fence, the space, and the bit widths are the same as the thickness of the mat material. Cut the cross grain grooves first. Use a backer piece of scrap material when making the cross grain cuts. This prevents chipping. (See figure 6–D–11). Make the first cut with the mat edge tight against the fence. Slip the first cut over the fence and make the second cut. Place the second cut over the fence to make the third cut and so on until one side of the mat board has all the cross grain dados completed. Flip the mat over and make lengthwise or straight grain dados in the other side of the mat. (See figure 6–D–12). Use the same fence method as for the cross grain dados. Where the dados cross one another the cuts have made holes. (See figure 6–D–13). This lattice pot mat may be sanded lightly and finished with a protective coat if desired. It makes a unique and effective hot pot mat.

Figure 6–D–11 Cut the cross grain dados first using a backer piece to prevent chipping.

Figure 6–D–12 Make straight grain dados in the other side.

Figure 6–D–10 Make a wooden hot pot mat.

Figure 6–D–13 Where dados cross one another, the cuts have made holes.

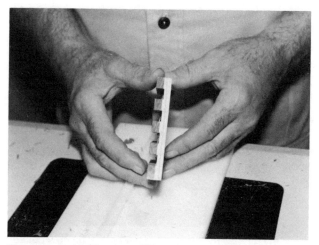

Figure 6–D–14 Glue two different woods together for novel effect lattice products.

For a novel effect, glue two contrasting woods together for pot mat stock. (See figure 6–D–14). Have the wood grain running one way on one side (walnut) and the opposite way on the other side (oak). Cut the pot mat the same as before only this time you will be making all straight grain cuts. This lattice piece will have walnut on one side and oak on the other. It is decorative as well as strong and warp free.

Using the above procedure, a number of other products may be constructed. Speaker cabinet fronts, ventilating grills, and decorative wall hangings can be made with this same lattice work procedure.

NOTE: Core box and provincial bits may also be used with the spacer fences.

Dovetailing with a Spacer Fence

Dovetail splicing and dovetail slides can be successfully constructed by using a ⅜'' spacer fence and a ½'' dovetail bit with a 14 degree angle. This dovetail bit has a taper from the wide ½'' end down the shank to about ¼''. Set the height of the bit up until the lower part of the dovetail portion of the bit is exactly ⅜'' wide and will easily fit over the ⅜'' spacer fence. (See figure 6–D–15). At this lower end the distance from the bit at the base to the fence should equal the ½'' bit size. Use a piece of sample stock and adjust the fence until you have a desired fit. Here again you will note that the greater the space between the bit and the fence the tighter the fit. The narrower the space between the bit and the fence the looser the fit.

For a dovetail splice it is necessary to have a tight fit. (See figure 6–D–16).

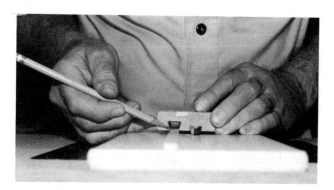

Figure 6–D–15 Set the dovetail bit the proper height.

Figure 6–D–16 Dovetail splice.

In constructing a dovetail slide a looser fit would be more desirable. (See figure 6–D–17).

This is an ideal joint to use when joining flat thin picture frame material at a 45 degree mitre. (See figure 6–D–18 and 6–D–19).

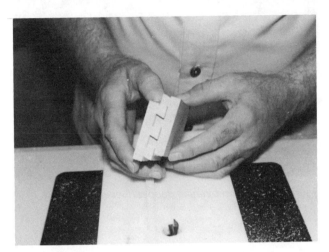

Figure 6–D–17 Dovetail slide.

Figure 6–D–18 Dovetail picture frame at 45 degree mitre.

Figure 6–D–19 Dovetail splice, 45 degree angle.

NOTE: When setting up your ⅜'' spacer fence to cut dovetails, you will notice that the fence must be further away from the bit, so you will have to elongate the bit hole in the fence. To do this, bolt one end of the fence (usually the back one) to the table, raise the bit to proper height (to leave ⅜'' wide slot at the bottom), start the router, and swing the fence out slightly allowing the bit to cut its own bit hole. (See figure 6–D–20).

Figure 6–D–20 Allow the bit to elongate the bit hole.

Secure the front table clamp. Once you get a desired fit on the dovetail splice, keep a sample set–up block for future operations. It will give you both the distance away from the fence and the height of the bit. This eliminates that constant measuring. Once set, you may like to drill a new hole for bolting the front of the fence to the router table.

Combination Dado–Rabbet Joint

Another joint that may be cut to perfection on a spacer fence is a combination dado and rabbet joint.

To set up, use a ⅜'' spacer fence with a ⅜'' straight bit set at ⅜'' depth of cut. Using ¾'' thick stock, run a ⅜'' wide and ⅜'' deep dado in the first piece. (See figure 6–D–21). Note that the dado is ⅜'' away from the edge. Slip this dado over the fence with the ⅜'' lip facing the cutter. Note that it will pass by the cutter without touching. Clamp the second piece of stock to the first piece (positioned over the fence) and slide it through the cutter. (See figure 6–D–22). Notice that the second piece has a ⅜'' by ⅜'' rabbet on its edge. Assemble the two pieces for a combination dado–rabbet corner joint that fits perfectly every time. (See 6–D–23).

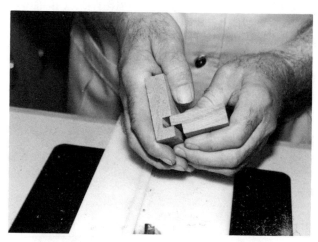

Figure 6–D–23 Combination dado rabbet corner joint.

Figure 6–D–21 Run a dado in the first piece of stock.

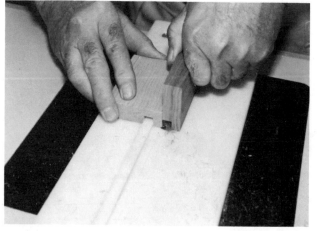

Figure 6–D–22 Cut a rabbet in the second piece as it is held snug against the dado piece.

Wooden Hinges

The spacer fence can be used for box joints which can be turned into wooden hinges by simply drilling a hole through the fingers and inserting either a wood dowel stick or a wire pin for the hinge to turn on.

E. Pattern Cutting with a Pattern Jig

Novel picture frames may be routed out of solid stock using a sliding pattern jig. The jig is designed to facilitate cutting a variety of designs and sizes of openings. Plastic blanks are available to enable the operator to draw, design, and cut patterns of his/her choice. (See figure 6–E–1).

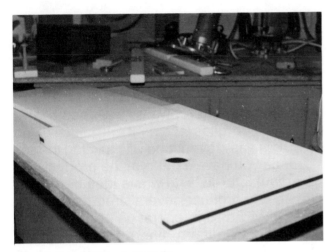

Figure 6–E–1 Use a pattern jig.

Making a Pattern

There are two methods for making a pattern. In the first method, slide the plastic blank into the jig and drill four registration holes in the blank to line the design cutout with the stock. Remove the plastic blank from the jig and cover the design area with masking tape. Draw or trace the desired design on the tape. Follow the drawn lines to cut the design out with the router. Use a ¼'' straight bit to cut the pattern.

NOTE: The design drawing must be larger than the product cutout by the distance from the outside edge of the bit to the outside edge of the template guide.

Smooth all the rough edges of the plastic pattern with a file. Remove the tape.

NOTE: As the finished product will only be as accurate as the jig pattern, take care to make a clean smooth job.

The second and probably the best method to make a pattern is to cut a master. Choose a piece of stock the size you wish or a size to fit the stock hole in the pattern jig. Because it is difficult to work on an inside pattern, it is best to cut the master stock in half lengthwise. Lay one half on top of the other and tape them together with masking tape. Trace or draw a half of the desired pattern on one side of the master stock. (See figure 6–E–2). Cut the pattern out and file the edges smooth. By cutting both halves at once you will be sure to have a true design with equal sides. Lay the two master halves out like a book, with the two pattern edges together. With masking tape, fasten the master pattern together in this position. (See figure 6–E–3).

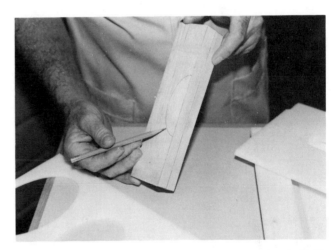

Figure 6–E–2 Make a master pattern by drawing half the pattern on the master stock.

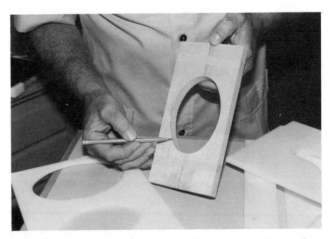

Figure 6–E–3 Tape the master with the two pattern edges together.

Insert the master in the pattern jig and slide the plastic blank over top. (See figure 6–E–4).

Use a pin to lock this piece in place to ensure that it does not move during the routing operation. The brass safety pin works great for this. Drill a ¾'' hole in the plastic blank anywhere in the pattern opening below. (See figure 6–E–5).

In the router mount a flush trim router bit that will go through the drilled hole that you made in the plastic blank. The pilot on the end of the bit will follow the master pattern. By routing around the entire pattern, you will have duplicated it in the plastic piece. (See figure 6–E–6).

The master may now be stored for future use in case the plastic pattern is damaged.

Figure 6–E–6 Rout a pattern from the master.

NOTE: The plastic I recommend for patterns is the ¼'' stress relieved polyethylene. It has a very slippery texture, wears well, and allows the router to glide across it with little or no drag. It is easy to rout and will not clog the bit.

Once you have a pattern, the product can be manufactured. The whole idea of pattern cutting is to produce several products exactly the same. For this operation you require a pattern jig, a pattern, and a template guide fastened in the router base plate. (See figure 6–E–7).

This template guide has a small flange protruding about ¼'' long. This flange follows the pattern while the bit is allowed to run freely inside the template without coming in contact with the pattern. Regardless of the pattern shape , the guide will follow it. Patterns must be larger than the finished product by the distance from the outside edge of the cutter to the outside edge of the template guide. (See figure 6–E–8).

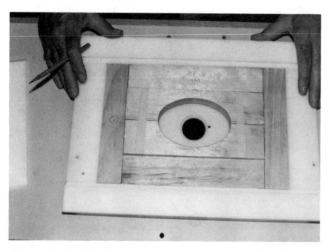

Figure 6–E–4 Centre the master in the pattern jig with filler blocks.

Figure 6–E–5 Lock the blank pattern piece over the master in the pattern jig.

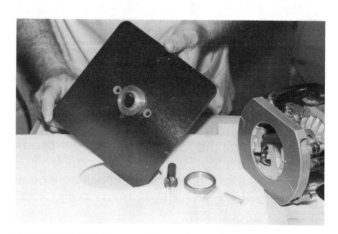

Figure 6–E–7 Pattern work requires a jig, a pattern, and a template guide mounted on the router base plate.

Figure 6-E-8 The pattern is bigger than the finished product.

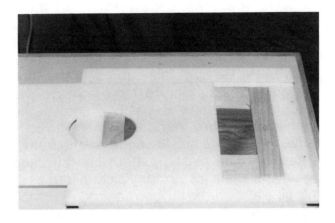

Figure 6-E-10 Slide the pattern over the stock.

Picture Frame

Lay the stock in the insert hole of the pattern jig. (See figure 6-E-9). Slide the oval plastic pattern over the stock. (See figure 6-E-10). Mount a decorative bit and a template guide in the router. Set the depth of cut to one half the stock thickness. Plunge the bit into the work piece and follow the pattern to cut the face side of the picture frame. (See figure 6-E-11).

Remove the pattern and the stock. Turn the stock over and lay it in the insert hole of the pattern jig. (See figure 6-E-12).

Figure 6-E-11 Cut the face side of the picture hole.

Figure 6-E-9 Lay the stock in the insert hole.

Figure 6-E-12 Turn the stock over and lay it in the pattern jig.

Slide the plastic pattern into place. Replace the decorative bit with a ¾'' straight bit. With the depth of cut set at one half the thickness of the stock, rout the design in the stock back. Be sure this cut meets the face side cut to free the picture frame from the oval cutout. (See figure 6–E–13). Remove the completed picture frame and apply a decorative mold to the outside edges of the frame, if desired. The plastic pattern can be used again and again for as many picture frames of this size and shape as are required. The face side of the picture frame has a decorative edge and the back side has a rabbeted recess to receive the picture. (See figure 6–E–14).

Figure 6–E–13 A rabbet in the back meets the decorative face side cut to free the picture hole plug.

Figure 6–E–14 The picture hole is cut. You may wish to mold the outside edges of the frame.

For different shape picture frames, make the desired design on a plastic blank to be used in the sliding pattern jig.

This versatile jig may be used for inlay cutting, dish routing, and picture/mirror framing.

F. Inlay Cutting

Recess and Inlay

We all admire professionally crafted inlays in furniture, novelties, and decorative products. One of the most difficult tasks is to cut a recess and then cut an inlay to fit perfectly into the recess. However, this becomes a simple operation with a plunge router, a straight bit, a template guide, and an inlay bushing. (See figure 6–F–1).

Make or choose a pattern. (See figure 6–F–2).

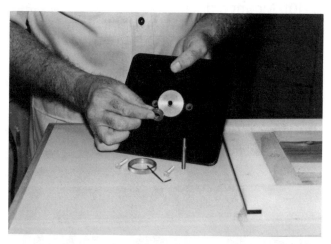

Figure 6–F–1 The inlay operation is done with a straight bit, a template guide, and an inlay bushing.

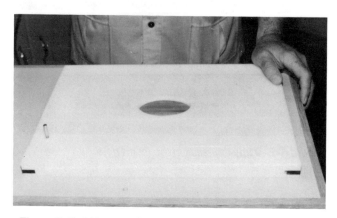

Figure 6–F–2 You need a pattern.

Using the inlay material for a guide, preset the depth of cut. (See figure 6–F–3). If using the pattern jig, slide the pattern over the material being used to receive the inlay. With bit, template guide, and inlay bushing in place on the router, cut a smooth clean recess in the material. Clean the recess by going back and forth with the router bit until the entire pattern area is recessed to the depth of the inlay material thickness. (See figure 6–F–4).

Remove the pattern and the recessed piece.

Remove the inlay bushing from the router. Tape the inlay material in the stock insert and position the pattern over it. (See figure 6–F–5). Cut the inlay material to the pattern shape being careful to follow the pattern outlines exactly. (See figure 6–F–6).

Figure 6–F–5 Tape the inlay material in the pattern jig.

Figure 6–F–3 Set the depth of cut.

Figure 6–F–6 Cut the inlay material.

Figure 6–F–4 Clean the recess in the material to receive the inlay.

Remove the pattern and the inlay cutout. The inlay should fit snugly into the recess. (See figure 6-F-7).

NOTE: The wall thickness of the bushing must be exactly the same as the width of the router bit. (See figure 6-F-8).

Figure 6-F-9 Make inlay butterflies in a contrasting wood.

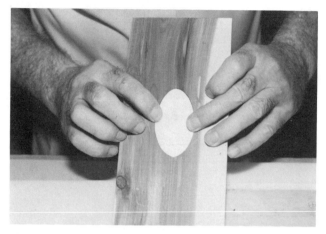

Figure 6-F-7 The inlay fits into the recess.

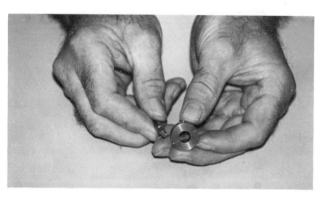

Figure 6-F-8 The bushing wall and the router bit width must be exactly equal.

NOTE: When you purchase a 1/4" router bit for inlay work, be sure that it is 1/4". Some manufacturers over-size their router bits and this would result in a poorly fitting inlay.

A prime application of the inlay procedure is the repair of a burnt spot in the plastic laminate of a table or counter top by inlaying a patch of the same laminate in place of the damaged spot. Patch a vinyl floor covering. Inlay butterflies in a floor or table top for decoration and strength. The butterflies can be made of a contrasting wood. (See figure 6-F-9).

Plaque Inlaying

Sometimes a ceramic plaque or china plate is to be inset flush into a table or mounting piece. This is easily accomplished using this same inlay method. Most times the outside edges of the plate or plaque will be uneven and irregular shaped. Therefore, the first step is to make a pattern. Using two sided tape, fasten the china plate or plaque to a 1/4" plastic pattern blank or 1/4" plywood. Securely clamp or fasten the blank or plywood to a backer board and work bench. With the inlay bushing removed and the 1/4" bit set deep enough to cut through the pattern material, let the template guide follow snugly around the plate or plaque. (See figure 6-F-10).

Figure 6-F-10 Make a pattern of the plague in 1/4" plywood.

Run the router from left to right. Fasten the pattern you have made to the table top or mounting piece. (See figure 6–F–11). Fasten the inlay bushing over the template guide on the router. Set the bit depth to accommodate the thickness of the plate, plaque, or inlay piece. (See figure 6–F–12).

Rout out the recess in the table top or mounting piece. (See figure 6–F–13). Clean the recess by moving the router bit back and forth across the pattern area. Because of its irregular shape the inlayed plate or plaque will probably fit in the recess only one way. Move it around the recess until it drops into place in a perfect fit. (See figure 6–F–14).

This method may be applied to any shape as long as the inlay bushing fits into the pattern.

NOTE: If large plates or plaques are used, a larger router base plate may be needed to span the distance across the pattern. The larger 11'' base plate works well for this. (See figure 6–F–15).

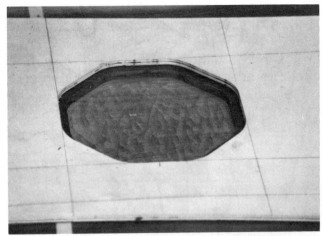

Figure 6–F–13 Rout the recess in the mounting piece.

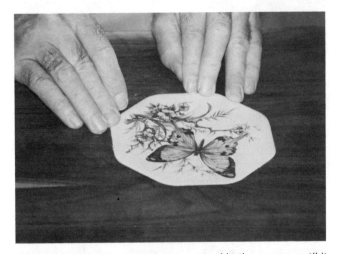

Figure 6–F–14 Move the plaque around in the recess until it drops into place.

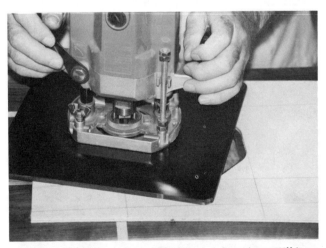

Figure 6–F–15 Some large patterns require a large 11'' base plate.

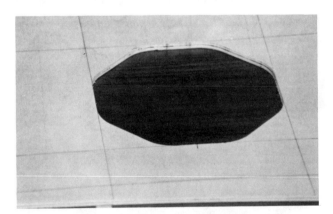

Figure 6–F–11 Tape the pattern to the mounting piece.

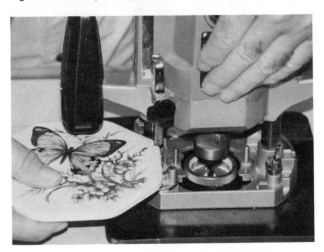

Figure 6–F–12 Set the depth of cut using the plaque.

G. Circle Cutting

It is difficult to cut a perfect circle. The difficult part is the free hand band saw cutting. Circle cutting can be simplified with a circle jig and a plunge style router. Several router attachments are available for circle cutting, but I find a circle jig is more versatile and easier to handle. Replace the router base plate with the circle jig. (See figure 6–G–1).

Secure the stock to a work bench. Choose a jig hole to correspond to the desired circle size. The radius will be the distance between the bit and the jig hole. Place this hole over the centre pin. (See figure 6–G–3). Plunge the router bit to a preset depth and rotate the router around the centre pin. The resulting circle is perfect every time. (See figure 6–G–4).

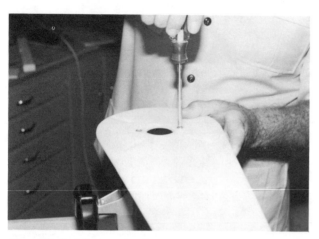

Figure 6–G–1 Secure the circle jig to the router.

Figure 6–G–3 Place the jig hole over the centre pin.

Locate and predrill a centre mark in the stock. Insert a centre pin. (See figure 6–G–2). To cut a circle that has no drill mark in the centre, simply tape a thumb tack up–side–down and use it as the centre pin. When the cut is complete remove the tape and tack. This can be done with a good deal of success because there is very little pull by the router in this operation.

Figure 6–G–4 Make perfect circles.

Figure 6–G–2 Locate and insert a centre pin.

74

Round Picture Frames

Using a centre pin and three or four jig holes, it is possible to make several round picture frames from one large piece of stock. (See figure 6–G–5). With a decorative bit mounted in the router, set the depth of cut at half the thickness of the stock. Clamp or fasten the stock to a work bench. The first cut will be the one closest to the centre pin. Determine the width of the picture frame desired. Add this amount to the first circle radius and place the chosen jig hole over the centre pin to make the second circle cut. Add the width of the picture frame to the second circle radius and place the chosen jig hole over the centre pin for a third cut. If the stock is large enough, make a fourth circle cut or simply use the square stock as a picture or mirror frame with a round cut out. This completes the decorative face cuts. (See figure 6–G–6).

Figure 6–G–6 Cut all the decorative face cuts first.

With the centre pin driven all the way through the stock, turn the stock over. Fasten the stock to a backer board with two way tape and clamp the backer board to a work bench. Using a plain mortising bit, repeat the circle cuts with the corresponding jig holes. For these cuts be sure to start with the outside cut first or the centre pin will be lost, making it impossible to complete the remaining cuts. Set the depth of cut to half the stock thickness. Be sure the mortise cut meets the decorative cut from the face side. (See figure 6–G–7). This mortise cut not only frees the circle frames but also provides a good rabbet for holding the picture or mirror in the back side of the frame.

Figure 6–G–5 Three circle cuts in each side of a large piece of stock produces three picture frames.

Figure 6–G–7 The mortise cuts in the back of the stock must meet the face side cuts.

To use the square outside stock as a frame with a round cut out, it may be necessary to mold the four outside edges with a decorative or rounding bit. It is possible to make decorative wood panels using the circle jig and geometric design knowledge. (See figure 6–G–8).

Figure 6–G–9 The bit must cut in wood on both sides of the cutter.

Figure 6–G–8 Geometric designs.

Round Tables

This method of circle cutting works extremely well when cutting large or small table tops. It is always a chore to hold a large wood table top up to the band saw, cut the circle, sand so there are no flat spots, and then mold the decorative edging. This entire operation can be completed with the circle jig. Install a rounding over plunge router bit and set the desired radius on the circle jig. Slip the jig over the centre pin or tack. Be sure that the bit is cutting in wood on both sides on all edges. This will prevent any pulling, chipping, or tear out. Never just trim the outside edge.(See figure 6–G–9).

Cut the face surface side first. (See figure 6–G–10). Then flip the table stock over and cut from the back side using the same procedure. Be sure the two cuts meet to free the table top from the scrap edge. The circular top will be perfectly round as well as completely molded. (See figure 6–G–11).

Figure 6–G–10 The face side is cut first.

Figure 6–G–11 The table top is cut and molded at the same time.

In the circle operation there is literally no pull by the router on the centre pin. Be sure to make the router work, do not take too many light cuts. I recommend the use of a one and one half horse power router with one pass on each side of the table top even if the stock is one and one half inches thick. This will result in a smoother cut. I am convinced that you will never free hand a circle or round table top again if you once try the above circle jig and router method. (See figure 6–G–12).

Figure 6–G–12 This table is about 5 feet in diameter.

Figure 6–H–1 Wood thread products.

H. Wood Threads

Threads are usually associated with metal screws and bolts. However, with a simple jig and the router, wood threads can be fashioned to make useful or novelty items. An oversized wooden bolt makes a novel paper weight. Wood clamps using threaded dowel pieces are a practical use for wood threading. (See figure 6–H–1). Wood threading is achieved with a router by using a simple jig and an angle bit. (See figure 6–H–2).

The jig consists of a wooden block with internal threads tapped part way through. There is space for a 60 degree angle plain router bit up the middle of the block. (See figure 6–H–3).

Figure 6–H–2 Wood thread jig with an angle bit.

Figure 6–H–3 The jig has tapped threads and a hole for the bit in the middle.

Securely fasten the jig to the router base. Slowly hand turn a given diameter dowel into the block jig with the router running. As the dowel crosses the bit a thread is started which engages with the tapped thread inside the jig. The cut thread pulls the dowel into the block jig while the router bit cuts matching external threads in the remaining dowel. (See figure 6–H–4). The external thread size is made to match the tapped thread in the jig.

NOTE: For wood threading use a dowel of very hard wood that has a tight grain, such as maple or purple heart.

Figure 6–H–4 Cutting wood threads in dowel.

Fashion wood bolts, wood clamps, and wood threaded dowels using this set up. They make excellent conversation pieces and novel gifts. (See figure 6–H–5).

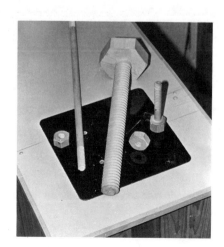

Figure 6–H–5 Wood bolts and threaded dowel.

The same block jig system works well for making doweling. Take a block of wood about 2 ½'' high by 4'' wide by 12'' long. On one side drill a 1'' hole half way through the block which would be 2'' deep. Change the drill size to ¾'' and continue drilling through the block. For example, to make ¾'' diameter doweling, the square strip would require a 1'' diameter hole, as this is the corner to corner measurement of a ¾'' by ¾'' square strip.

On the bottom side of the block drill a ¾'' hole up to meet the two side holes. Do not make this hole any deeper than just to meet the dowel holes. Mount a ¾'' template guide into the router table base plate. Mount a ½'' to ⅝'' straight two flute bit in the table mounted router. Place the block jig over the template guide using the bottom ¾'' hole. (See figure 6–H–6). Make sure the guide is fastened with the ring nut.

Raise the bit just enough to come flush with the bottom of the dowel size hole. Start the router and slowly feed the square strip through the 1'' hole. (See figure 6–H–7).

Rotate it until it emerges from the other hole as round dowel. (See figure 6–H–8).

Make a tight or loose fit by raising or lowering the bit. For other size dowel repeat the above setup. They may even be done in the same block.

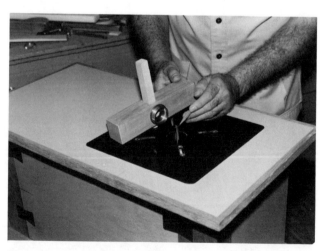

Figure 6–H–6 The dowel jig fits over a 3/4'' template guide.

Figure 6–H–7 Feed the square stock into the dowel jig.

Figure 6–H–8 Round dowel emerges from the other end.

Figure 6–I–1 Install a 3/4" template guide in the base plate.

I. Mitre jig

A table mounted router is versatile. It is made even more versatile with the use of a mitre jig. I have seen many types of router mitre jigs which try to duplicate the table saw mitre set up. I have never been pleased with this method for the router because the slot is so far removed from the base plate. I have designed a router mitre gauge that solves many problems. The best feature is that it is always in line with the bit regardless of how you hold it, run it, or turn it.

On a table mounted router install a ¾" brass template guide in the phenolic base plate. (See figure 6–I–1). Use any two fluted straight router bit or dovetail bit, that will run freely without touching the template guide. This jig has a slot that fits over the template guide allowing the jig to ride smoothly back and forth. Set the depth of cut, clamp the stock in place on the jig, and slide the jig forward over the bit. The bit is cutting in the centre of the template guide. This results in a clean cut, straight dado even if the jig is not kept in a straight line. (See figure 6–I–2).

Figure 6–I–2 Use the mitre jig at any angle.

This jig is ideal for cutting linear dovetails used in drawer construction. While it is quite easy to run a through dovetail using the router table and a fence, it is quite a different task to run stop dovetails in drawer fronts. If you were to use the fence you can mill the first one to a depth and stop block. But when it comes to run the opposite end, you must back up against the bit rotation and this is a practice I never recommend. With the mitre jig it is easy to simply lock the drawer front to the jig and run the first slot to a preset distance. Release the clamp and slide the drawer front to the right. Lock it in place and run the second slot. You have both stopped slots without having to run one in reverse. (See figures 6–I–3 and 6–I–4).

To complete the operation you require dovetail pins to be cut on each end of the drawer sides. Dovetail pins can be cut by using the table fence. Success with this method depends on each piece being exactly the same thickness or the pins could be of different width. Using the mitre jig and attachment results in perfect fit with little set up. Using the right angle stop block prelocated on the mitre jig, clamp the drawer side on end. Make the first cut. (See figure 6–I–5). With the drawer side still clamped securely to the right angle block move the block to the second preset locating pin and cut the other side of the pin.

Figure 6–I–3 Run stopped dovetails into a drawer front.

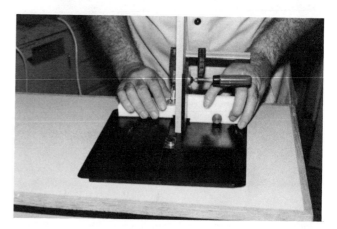

Figure 6–I–5 Make one side of the drawer side dovetail pin by using the right angle stop block on the mitre jig.

Because of the preset locating pins the dovetail pin on the end of the drawer side will be a perfect fit regardless of the thickness of the material. (See figure 6–I–6 and 6–I–7).

Figure 6–I–4 Cut both dovetail slots without having to run one in reverse.

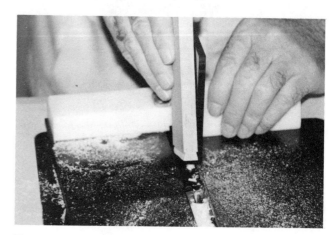

Figure 6–I–6 A perfect dovetail pin.

NOTE: Remember do not change the height of the bit from the preset depth of cut for slots or pins.

By changing the angle block to a 45 degree angle, the diagonal corner blocks with the 45 degree pins can be cut for the leg and rail construction. (See figure 6–I–8 and 6–I–9).

Figure 6–I–7 Fit the drawer side and front together.

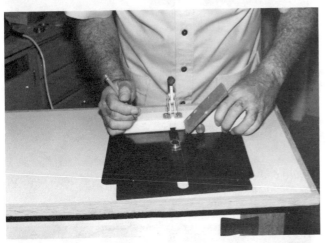

Figure 6–I–8 Use a 45 degree angle block.

Figure 6–I–9 Dovetail 45 degree corner blocks for leg construction.

J. Repeat Dado Fence

When you constructed storage shelving or cabinet shelves, a number of dados are required to install the shelves. The trick is to get all the shelves evenly spaced and level. Most times this may be done by measuring and using a straight edge, but sometimes, by the time the cabinet side is done, the shelves slope one way or the other. This fence eliminates the measuring and cuts down on the errors.

Most router bases are milled to receive a fence which consists of a block and two rods that are adjustable on the base. (See figure 6–J–1). To make the dado fence use two short rods of any length. The diameter should fit the holes in the base. Thread one end of each rod down about 2''. Use a small block of wood or polyethylene about 1'' wide and 8'' long. Drill two holes in the block to match the spacing of the rods when attached to the router base. The thickness of the block must match the width of the dado bit being used. You may like to make several different size fences in a variety of thicknesses. (See figure 6–J–2).

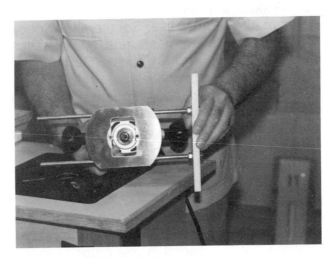

Figure 6–J–1 Make a dado fence.

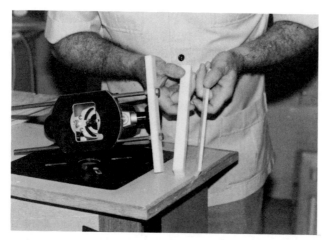

Figure 6-J-2 Make dado blocks in different sizes to fit the same fence.

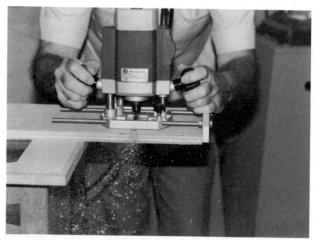

Figure 6-J-3 Run the first dado.

NOTE: The block must be the same width as the bit to allow the block to slide freely into the dado groove.

Lock the block between two nuts on each rod. Slide the other two ends into the fence holes on the router base. Set the shelf spacing you require by measuring the distance between the bit and the block. Be sure the fence is mounted on the left side of the router. (Check direction of feed instructions). Set the depth of cut and with the fence hanging over the left end of the shelving side, cut the first dado. (See figure 6-J-3). Move the router down and allow the block to slide in the first dado. Cut the second dado. (See figure 6-J-4).

Repeat this procedure until you have completed the shelving side. Using the same method cut the dados in the other shelving side. The spacing between the shelves will be exactly the same and the two sides will match perfectly with little or no measuring. (See figure 6-J-5).

Figure 6-J-4 Slide the dado block in the first dado and cut the second dado.

Figure 6-J-5 Cut dados for shelves without measuring.

Unit 7
Construction Routing

A. Industry

Routers are used extensively in the construction and prefab industries for cutting electrical and mechanical outlets, window openings, door openings, form work, scribing, panelling, trimming, setting moldings, and glazing. The mobile home industry, recreation vehicle industry and floor covering industry have been well served by routers. Most of these industry routers are air routers meant for line production. Industry does not use small home utility routers.

Figure 7–A–1 A panel cutting bit with a spear point is used to cut window/door openings in sheathing.

In a mobile home plant routers would be used to cut through metal cladding and sheathing in one operation to make an opening for a door or window. This use is now seen in smaller on site construction where the studs, plates, and rough framed openings are placed, the sheathing is nailed over the entire wall section, and then the router is used with a panel cutting, spear point bit to make the openings in the sheathing. (See figure 7–A–1). The depth of cut is preset to cut through the sheathing material. The panel bit is plunged into the framed opening and guided along the rough framing of the window and door openings. It takes seconds to cut the openings. (See figure 7–A–2). On the gable ends the router works well to trim the sheathing flush with the framing. This is much easier and more accurate than trying to precut the sheathing prior to nailing it on the gable. One of the unique things about using a router for this operation is that when cutting it does not bind or kick back like a hand electric saw. The router out performs the saw for speed and quality fit.

Figure 7–A–2 The router cuts openings in seconds.

B. Matching Jointing and Scribing

A sign of quality in any woodworking project is perfectly fitted joints and splices. This is a difficult task when the worker must scribe wood panelling to fit along a stone fireplace; or when the worker must match uneven edges of panelling, laminate, or veneer; or when the worker must joint or square up an uneven panel edge. Traditionally, all these jobs were painstakingly done by hand. With modern routers, the same procedures can be done perfectly in a fraction of the time.

Jointing Panels and Laminates

Panelling almost always arrives with uneven factory edges. In bringing two panels together to make a satisfactory butt joint, clamp the two panels firmly onto a backing board. A piece of plywood, heavy enough to support the panelling and the router, makes a good backing board. To correct uneven edges of panelling clamp a straight edge parallel to the joint and set a distance away to allow the router base to follow the straight edge while the bit must run in the centre of the joint. (See figure 7–B–1). A quarter inch straight bit works well for this operation. Set the depth of cut to slightly deeper than the thickness of the panelling. This will leave a slight groove in the backing board when the cut is made.

Figure 7–B–1 Straighten panelling with a router and a straight edge.

If the bit width removes too much material from the panel, space the panels slightly apart before making the cut. The two panels will now have smooth even edges that should match perfectly.

Joint and splice plastic laminate and veneer with this same method.

A similar method is used to fit and match laminates applied in a corner. Usually a counter corner is not square. When covering an uneven corner with laminate lay the sheets overlapped in the corner. Place each sheet parallel to its respective wall. The unevenness of the corner angle will have no bearing on the splice. Mark the locations on each sheet so they may be moved to a work bench and realigned in position. (See figure 7–B–2).

Figure 7–B–2 Mark the laminate as it fits a corner counter. Remove and realign the laminate on a work bench.

Using the jointing method with a straight edge and the router, cut through both laminate sheets from corner to corner. (See figure 7–B–3). Remove the scrap ends and slide the laminate pieces into position on the counter. This makes a perfect splice. (See figure 7–B–4).

NOTE: When making this cut keep in mind that the length allowance for the counter must include the width of cut lost in making the splice.

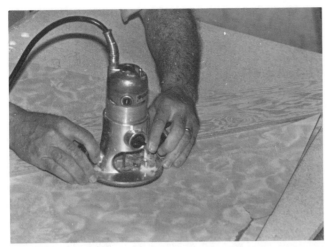

Figure 7–B–3 Using a straight edge, cut the laminate from corner to corner.

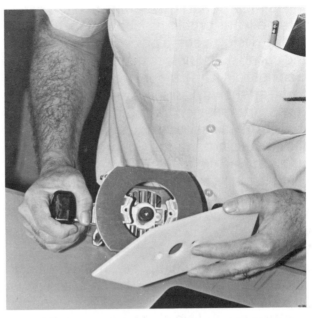

Figure 7–B–5 Attach the scribing jig to the router base plate.

Figure 7–B–4 The laminate matches perfectly in the corner.

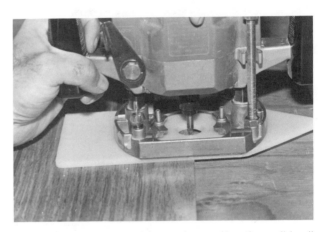

Figure 7–B–6 The router bit cuts the panel as the scribing jig follows an uneven surface.

Scribing

A simple scribing jig can be made to fasten to the router base. (See figure 7–B–5). When fitting panelling to an uneven corner or surface, this jig does a good scribing job. Mount the panelling on the wall parallel to the corner and a distance away that will allow the jig point to follow the uneven corner surface while the router bit contacts the panelling for the entire cut. Use a ¼'' straight bit. Depth of cut should be set to cut through the panelling. Follow the corner or uneven surface with the jig point as you cut the panelling with the router bit. The panel cut will match the corner or uneven surface exactly. (See figure 7–B–6). Use the same jig to scribe counter topping to fit against an uneven wall.

C. Electrical Outlet

Cutting wall material to receive electrical outlets is always a frustrating experience because the outlets are irregular in shape and sometimes they are installed in a crooked position.

A traditional method has been to chalk the outlets, lay the panelling in place and hope the chalk shows on the back of the panel. The other traditional method is to take a series of measurements to be transferred to the panel. This method often results in the outlet being cut in the wrong place, for example, in the top instead of the bottom, on the right side instead of the left side.

A simple outlet jig used with a router eliminates all the problems connected to outlet cutting. Using a scrap piece of plywood, mark and cut an outlet hole to match the outlet box. (See figure 7–C–1). Mount two aligning pins in the jig as shown or use two way tape. All outlet boxes are installed to protrude beyond the stud by the thickness of the wall material. This allows you to hang the jig in place over the outlet box. (See figure 7–C–2). Put the panelling in place over the jig and push in tightly against the jig. This causes the aligning pins to secure the jig to the back of the panelling or wall material. If two way tape is used press tightly enough to ensure the tape sticks to the wall material fastening the jig to the back. Remove the panelling and place it face down on the work bench. Be sure the jig is taped or clamped securely in place, before routing.

In the router, mount a panel bit with a spear point and pilot. Set the depth of cut to slightly more than the thickness of the panelling. Cut the outlet following the jig pattern. (See figure 7–C–3). The router bit rotation makes a smooth cut without splintering the face side of the panelling. Saws often splinter the panelling.

Remove the jig and fasten the panelling or wall material in place. Notice the snug splinter–free fit around the outlet box.(See figure 7–C–4).

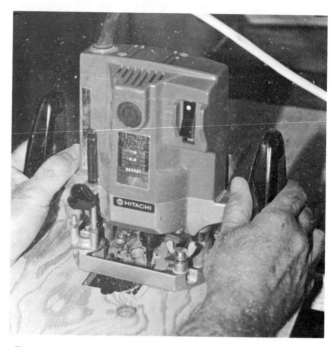

Figure 7–C–3 Follow the jig pattern to cut the outlet in the panelling.

Figure 7–C–1 Electrial outlet jig.

Figure 7–C–2 Hang the jig over the outlet box.

Figure 7–C–4 The panelling is spliner free and snug around the outlet box.

Figure 7–D–1 The open and housed stringers in this curved stair case were cut with a router.

D. Stairs

Stairs with housed stringers have always been left to manufacturers and skilled carpenters. (See figure 7–D–1). With a router this operation may be performed with a high degree of accuracy, using a manufactured jig or a shop made jig. (See figure 7–D–2 and figure 7–D–3).

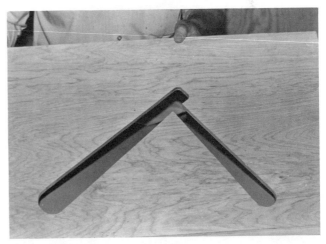

Figure 7–D–3 Shop made stair jig.

Figure 7–D–2 Manufactured stair jig.

The term 'housed stringer' implies that the risers and treads are mortised into the stringer. (See figure 7-D-4). The jig can be a very simply constructed one that allows the operator to cut both gains for the riser and the tread at one setting. The size of the gains makes allowance for a wedge to be driven in behind each riser and beneath each tread. (See figure 7-D-5). This method eliminates the need for any mechanical fastening. With these stair jigs use a template guide and a mortising bit mounted in the router. (See figure 7-D-6). It is not necessary for these gains to be more than one half inch deep.

The jig must be reversible as it is necessary to make one left hand and one right hand stringer for each set of stairs. The jig will allow adjustment to any given rise size and tread size.

Figure 7-D-5 Wedges are driven behind each riser and beneath each tread.

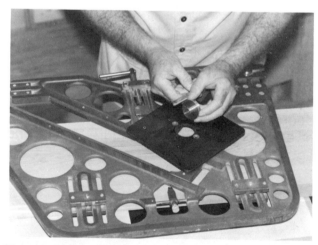

Figure 7-D-6 For routing stairs you require a jig, a template guide, and a mortising bit.

Figure 7-D-4 A housed stringer means the risers and treads are mortised into the stringers.

E. Hinge Jig

If you have to make a large number of hinge mortises, it will probably pay to purchase a butt template jig. This jig is designed for setting two or three hinge mortises on any normal size door. It is adjustable to handle hinge sizes from three inches to five inches. Illustrations and step-by-step procedures of only one manufactured jig are discussed here. (See figure 7-E-1). Most manufactured jigs will have similar components and a complete set of instructions. Be sure to follow the manufacturers instructions.

Figure 7-E-1 Manufactured hinge jig.

This kit consists of three template sections and two adjustment bars. (See figure 7-E-2). When properly assembled, it will be possible to cut out one, two, or three identical hinge gains in several doors and jambs without resetting the jig.

Figure 7-E-2 The jig consists of three template sections and two adjustment bars.

In this example, we will set three butt hinges (3 ½'' x 3 ½'') in a standard size door (6'8'' high and 1 ¾'' thick). Note that the width of the door has nothing to do with the hinge set up. Determine the length and thickness of the door. Each template section has two door thickness locating pins, one at each end. (See figure 7-E-3). Set the thickness locating pins to correspond with the door thickness on all three template sections. (See figure 7-E-4).

Figure 7-E-3 Arrows point to door thickness pins in the template section.

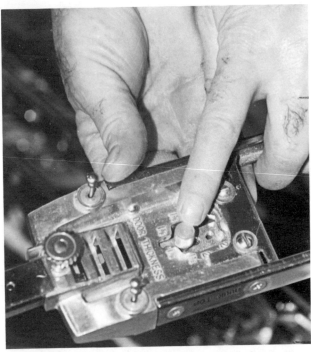

Figure 7-E-4 The thickness pins must be set to correspond with the door thickness.

On the side of each template section there is a hinge length adjustment scale which consists of a series of paired holes. (See figure 7–E–5). There is a round locating pin that should be removed and set in the pair of holes that correspond to the desire hinge size. In this example they would be set in the 3 ½'' holes. Set the locating pins in all three template sections. (See figure 7–E–6).

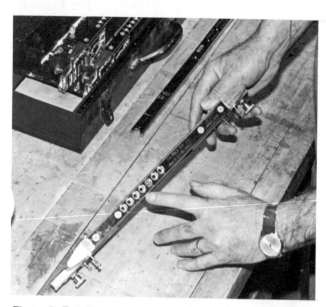

Figure 7–E–5 The hinge length adjustment scale is located on each side of the template sections.

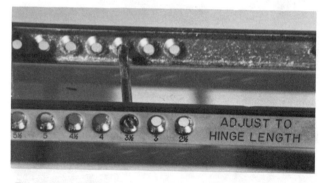

Figure 7–E–6 Set the hinge length at 3 1/2'' by positioning the locating pin in the proper pair of holes. Do this on all three template sections.

Assembling the Jig

One of the three templates has a top-of-the-door-adjusting-bar indicating the numbers; 5'', 6'', and 7''. This bar also has a clearance gage at the top which adjusts from left to right. (See figure 7–E–7). For our example, this clearance gage is locked in at 7'' which is the standard location for a top hinge.

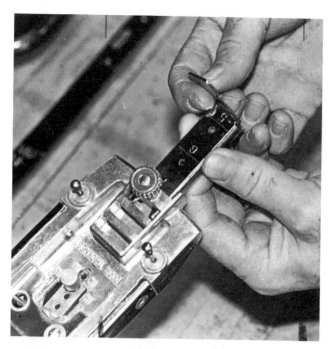

Figure 7–E–7 The clearance gage on the top template section adjusts to left or right.

Select an adjusting bar and insert it into the bottom end of the top template. Lock it in place at the proper door length (6'8''). (See figure 7–E–8). Note the indications and scales on the bar.(See figure 7–E–9). Insert the other end of this bar into either of the remaining templates being sure the arrow directions indicating the door top are placed correctly.

Figure 7–E–8 Lock the adjusting bar into the top template section at the proper door height.

Figure 7–E–9 Door height scales are indicated on the adjusting bar.

Using the 7–11 scale, lock the bar into the template at the 3 ½'' hinge length shown on the adjusting bar. (See figure 7–E–10). Repeat this procedure for the remaining bar and template.

Figure 7–E–11 Complete the jig set–up.

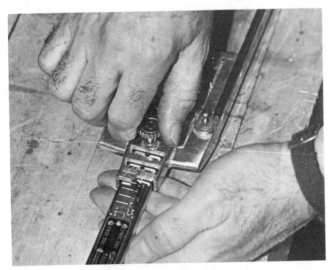

Figure 7–E–10 Insert the bottom of the adjusting bar into one of the remaining template sections.

The jig is now ready to be attached to the door. (See figure 7–E–11). Determine if the door is to be a right or left swing. Using a sash and door holder, stand the door on edge with the hinge side up. Hook the clearance gage over the top of the door according to either the right or left swing. (See figure 7–E–12). Ensure that the thickness pins are snug against the door edge.

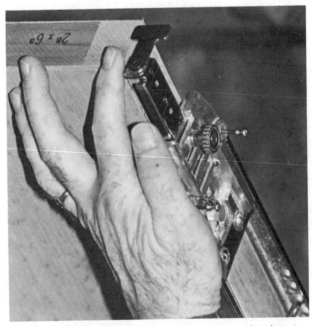

Figure 7–E–12 Hook the clearance gage over the door top.

NOTE: Each template has four spring loaded nailing pins designed to hold the jig in place while the gains are routed. (See figure 7–E–13).

Drive the nailing pins into the door to secure the jig.

Figure 7–E–13 Each template section has four nailing pins to hold the jig on the door.

Router Setup

> CAUTION: The router is unplugged and the motor switch is in the 'OFF' position.

Install the hinge template guide in the router base. (See figure 7–E–14). Mount a hinge mortising bit in the router chuck. (See figure 7–E–15). Tighten the collet. Use the hinge to adjust the depth of cut to the proper hinge depth. (See figure 7–E–16).

Figure 7–E–14 Hinge template guide.

Figure 7–E–15 Hinge mortising bit.

Figure 7–E–16 Adjust the depth of cut by using the hinge to measure.

With the motor switch at 'OFF' connect the plug to the power outlet. Position the router bit in the template opening away from the door. Turn the motor switch to 'ON' and let the router come to full power before starting the cut. To prevent chipping, score the right hand end of the gain. Back the bit out. (See figure 7–E–17). Starting at the left hand side of the gain, cut the outside edges of the gain following the template. Working from left to right, clean up the gain with the router. Position the bit in the template opening away from the door and turn the motor switch to 'OFF'.

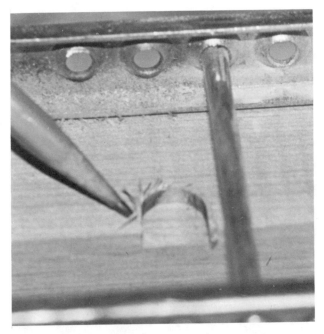

Figure 7–E–17 Score the right hand end of the gain.

Repeat the above procedure in the two remaining templates to finish the three hinge gains in the door. Remove the jig from the door.

NOTE: The routed gains have two inside corners that are rounded because of the mortising bit. If matching hinges are not available, this small radius may have to be squared with a hand wood chisel. (See figure 7–E–18).

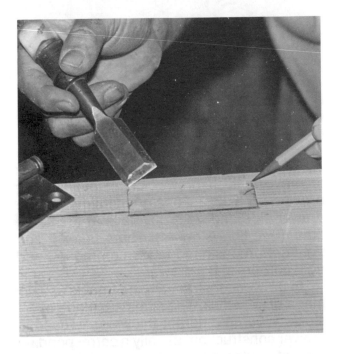

Figure 7–E–18 Square the rounded corners with a hand wood chisel.

To make corresponding gains in the jamb, install the jig on the hinge side of the jamb with the clearance gage butted snugly against the header.

NOTE: The clearance gage thickness is designed to allow door swing clearance.

Following the same router procedure used with the door, cut hinge gains in the jamb. Be sure the set up is correct for the proper left or right door swing. (See figure 7–E–19).

All doors and jambs with these same hinge and door specifications can now be routed without resetting the jig.

Figure 7–E–19 Cut corresponding hinge gains in the door jamb using the same jig set-up.

F. Dovetail Jig

The strongest wood joint is the dovetail. These joints have gained the distinction of being a sign of quality. In the past, intricate joints like the dovetail were left to the experienced cabinet maker. Now the dovetail can be easily constructed with a router and a template jig. Dovetail jigs are inexpensively manufactured by most power tool firms.

The set up for one manufactured jig is discussed here in a step by step format. (See figure 7–F–1). Most dovetail jigs will have corresponding components and a set of instructions. It is a wise idea to read the instructions which are enclosed with each template jig to insure proper assembly. Jigs may vary with the manufacturer.

Figure 7–F–2 Clamp the jig to a work bench.

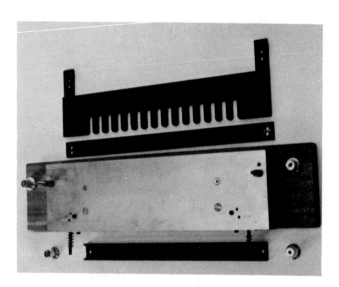

Figure 7–F–1 Manufactured dovetail jig.

Figure 7–F–3 Note the aligning pins. Be sure they are in matched positions at both left and right sides of the jig.

The base plate of the jig should be fastened to a block of wood or plywood which can be clamped to a work bench or fastened in a bench vise. (See figure 7–F–2).

Check the aligning pins on both the right and left sides, to see that they are in a matched position. (See figure 7–F–3). These aligning pins make the necessary offset between the front and side of the drawer.

The pin arrangement allows the operator to make a flush drawer or an overlapping drawer. The jig is designed to make the drawer side and front dovetails at the same time. (See figure 7–F–4). There is a left and right set up designed to fashion the left and right corners of the drawer.

In drawer construction, the front is usually made of 3/4'' stock. The sides are made of 1/2'' stock. When a different thickness is used in drawer construction, usually a corresponding size of router bit, template, and finger jig would also be needed.

Figure 7–F–4 Dovetails are made in the drawer front and side at the same time.

Using standard drawer stock, as indicated above, mount the drawer side against the left hand aligning pin under the front clamping bar and slightly (¼'') above the base plate. (See figure 7–F–5). Temporarily snug the side into place by tightening the front clamping bar.

Lay the drawer front face down and flat on the base plate. Ease it against the aligning pin and position it snugly against the extended drawer side. Notice that the drawer front and side are offset. (See figure 7–F–6).

Place the finger plate and the top clamping bar in place over the drawer front. Tighten the top clamping bar to hold the front in place.

Loosen the front clamping bar and raise the drawer side to make it flush with the drawer front and tight against the under side of the jig fingers. (See figure 7–F–7). Tighten

the front clamping bar to hold the side in place. Check both clamping bars. They must be tight to hold the pieces in place during the routing operation. (See figure 7–F–8).

Figure 7–F–6 The drawer side and front are off-set.

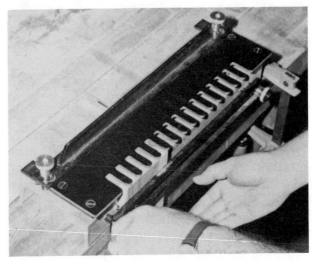

Figure 7–F–7 Make sure the drawer side is positioned tight against the under side of the jig fingers.

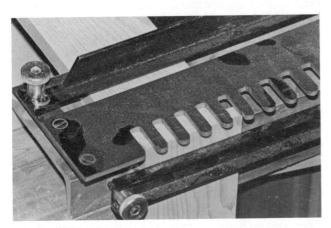

Figure 7–F–5 Position the drawer side behind the front clamping bar and snug against the aligning pin.

Figure 7–F–8 Check both clamping bars to be sure they are tight.

Check the dovetail template guide to see that it fits snugly into the finger slots of the jig. (See figure 7–F–9).

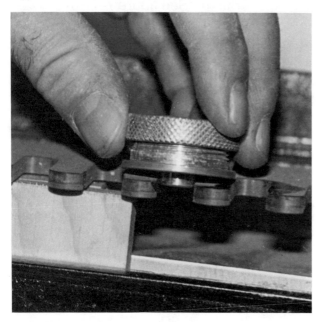

Figure 7–F–9 The dovetail template must fit the finger slots of the jig exactly.

CAUTION:The router is unplugged and the motor switch is in the 'OFF' position.

Mount the template guide on the router base plate. Mount the ½'' dovetail bit through the template guide and into the router collet. (See figure 7–F–10). Tighten the bit into place. NOTE: The large diameter of the bit cannot pass through the template guide. Be sure that the bit does not ride on the guide. It must turn freely inside the guide. (See figure 7–F–11).

The crucial measurement in the dovetail operation is the depth of cut. The dovetail bit should extend $^{19}/_{32}$'' beyond the router base. If the joint is too loose, slightly lower the bit until a snug joint is accomplished. If the joint is too tight, slightly raise the bit until the fit is perfect. Always try joints and cuts on scrap stock to test the fit before routing the project pieces.

CAUTION: Be sure the router base is kept tightly against the template fingers during the routing operation. Because the dovetail bit flares out below the template, any motion upwards while routing the finger slots will cause the bit to chip and ruin the finger guide.

Figure 7–F–11 Check the dovetail bit to be sure it is not riding on the guide.

Figure 7–F–10 Mount a 1/2'' dovetail bit through the template guide into the router chuck and tighten it in.

With the motor switch in the 'OFF' position, connect the router to an electrical outlet. Firmly gripping the handles of the router, turn the motor switch to 'ON' and let the router reach full power before starting the cut. Make test pieces with scrap stock first.

To prevent inside chipping of the drawer side, make a scoring cut in the outside edge of the drawer side by holding the router base flat on the template guide and cutting parallel from left to right in front of the jig fingers. (See figure 7–F–12).

When this is complete go back to the left hand notch. Proceed to rout in and out of each finger and along the front following the outline of the template jig. (See figure 7–F–13). The dovetails in the side and front pieces are completed. Test for fit. (See figure 7–F–14).

Figure 7–F–12 Score the drawer side all along in front of the jig fingers.

Figure 7–F–13 Rout in and out the jig fingers from left to right.

Insert the other end of the drawer front next to the right aligning pin of the template. Match the right hand drawer side against it on the right apron. Repeat the dovetail operation as before making dovetails in the right hand side and front.

Figure 7–F–14 Test the completed dovetail joint for fit.

This completes the dovetails for the construction of one drawer. Make as many drawers as the plan calls for without changing the jig.

Unit 8
Joinery

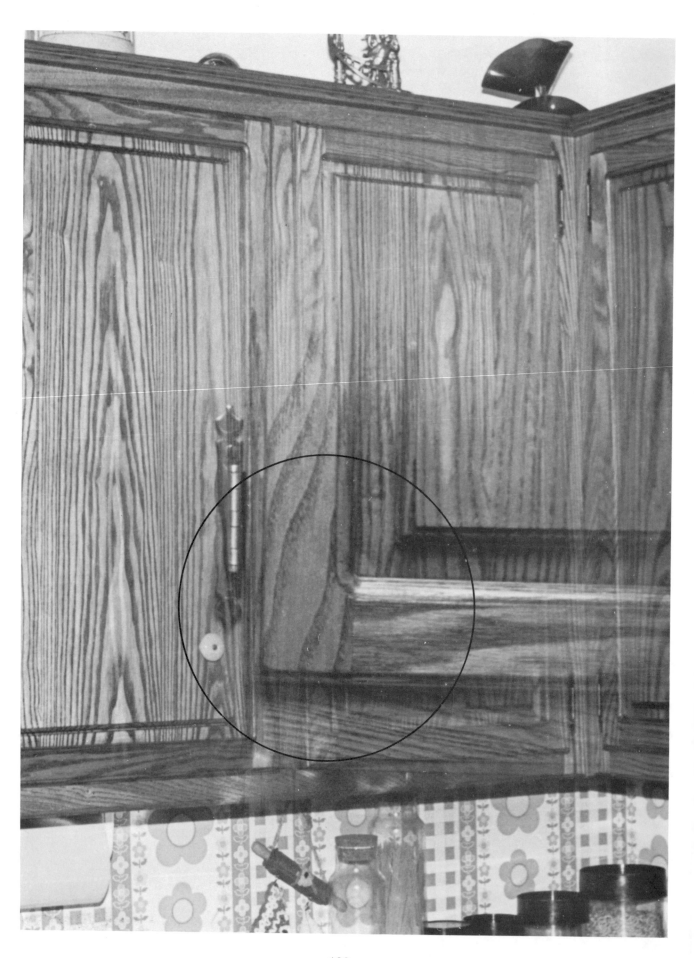

A. Wood Joints

There are well over a hundred different kinds of wood joints used by industry in construction and furniture manufacturing. Some joints are very complicated. They require either a special machine or a great deal of skill. Others are basic and simple. The most important consideration is to choose the simplest joint that will do the job the best.

Many wood joints are easily made with a router. Plan simple layouts to improve quality. The art of joinery is the skill to assemble and fasten two or more pieces of stock together in a neat strong fashion to give the impression that they 'grew there'.

Figure 8–A–1 Footstool leg joint.

Leg And Rail Joint

When it comes to mounting a leg on a table or stool, strength must be the first consideration. The best method that I recommend is butting the leg into the corner of the rails and using a hanger bolt across the corner. Industry has used this method for years with great success. In most cases they use a metal plate across the corner. But a wooden block works just as well. (See figure 8–A–1).

Cut the legs and rails to the desired size. Then cut the corner blocks to fit. They should be the same width as the rails. To find the proper length just figure two times the leg width. For example, if the leg is 2'' by 2'', the corner blocks will be 4'' long. The notch in the rails is cut by using a 90 degree V groove bit. This operation can be done on the router table using the mitre jig. See Mitre jig in Unit 6. The distance this notch is set back from the end of the rail is the width of the leg. If the leg is 2'' by 2'' the set back is 2''. Screw the blocks in the corners, mount the hanger bolt into the corner of the leg, and bolt it in place. Attach all four legs in this manner.

Figure 8–A–2 Make 45 degree dovetails in the corner blocks.

Another method of using a wooden corner block is to dovetail the corner block into the rail. (See figure 8–A–2). Refer to the section on the mitre jig for details on how to construct the dovetails. The same method is used to determine the length and set back of the blocks. Always check for accuracy by using scrap material before cutting into the project stock. You may wish to allow a different margin between the leg and the rail.

Corner Dovetail and Spline

This joint is not only decorative but it can provide a great deal of strength and it is quite easy to do. (See figure 8–A–3). Mitre the corner of the project at a 45 degree angle. This is best done with a 45 degree chamfer bit. Next determine the thickness of the spline. The spline slot can be cut right through or blind. A slot cutter of the spline thickness works well for this. Keep in mind when making the spline that the direction of the grain must be across the grain not with it. Now glue the corner with the spline in place putting the dovetail through the corner. This operation is best done on a router table. However, if the project is too large, a V block jig can be used. (See figure 8–A–4 and 8–A–5).

For a smaller project, mount the dovetail bit in the table mounted router. Determine the fence distance from the bit. Using a V block to hold the mitre corner cut the dovetail slots. Do not change the height of the bit. Move the fence and cut a linear dovetail pin to fit snugly in the dovetail slots. (See figure 8–A–6).

Slide the pin into the slot, glue, and trim flush. A contrasting wood makes a very decorative joint. These dovetails can be applied evenly or randomly to the joint.

With a little modification, this joint can become a locked corner. Simply make the spline thicker and let the dovetail pins penetrate part way into the splines.

Figure 8–A–5 Through dovetail slot.

Figure 8–A–3 Corner dovetail spline.

Figure 8–A–6 Make a dovetail pin to fit the slot.

Figure 8–A–4 On a large product, fasten the jig to the corner and rout the dovetail with a hand held router.

Dovetail Splines

Sometimes a dovetail spline can be used to fasten a mitred corner. They may be used on edge or on the flat. (See figure 8-A-7).

Cut the dovetail slot in the mitre. The simplest way to cut the dovetail spline is to use a bit that is designed for that purpose. You must always have the grain run across the joint. Cut these on the end of a ½'' piece of stock and then cut them to the proper length. Glue and insert the spline in the mitre.

The following photographs show wood joints that can be produced with a router. (See figures 8-A-8 to 8-A-21).

Figure 8-A-9 Spline.

Figure 8-A-7 Dovetail splines in a mitred corner joint.

Figure 8-A-10 Combination spline and open dovetail.

Figure 8-A-8 Finger joints.

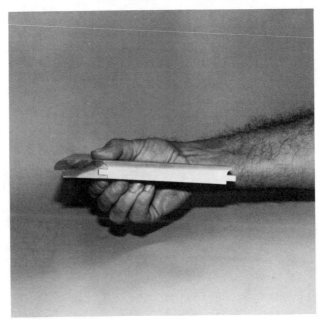

Figure 8-A-11 Cope and bead for slide and rail.

Figure 8–A–12 Glue joint.

Figure 8–A–15 Box joint.

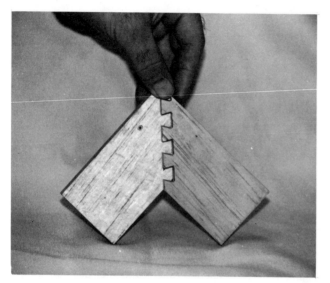

Figure 8–A–13 Dovetail on 45 degree angle.

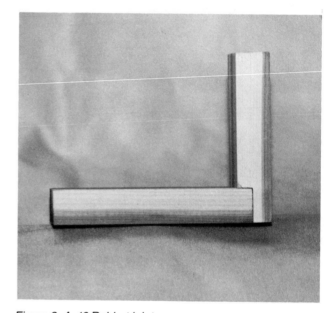

Figure 8–A–16 Rabbet joint.

Figure 8–A–14 Dado.

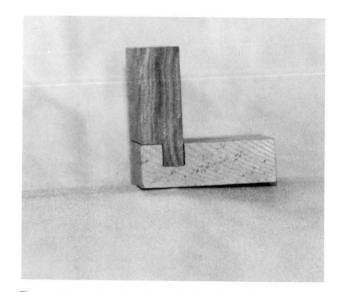

Figure 8–A–17 Combination rabbet and dado joint.

Figure 8–A–18 Sliding dovetail.

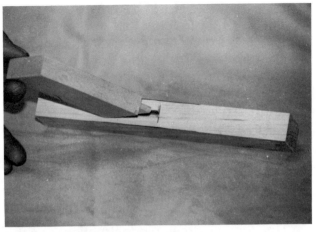

Figure 8–A–20 Mortise and tenon.

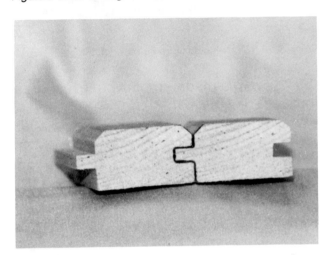

Figure 8–A–19 Tongue and Groove "V" joint.

Figure 8–A–21 Panel splice.

B. Dovetail Drawers

It is generally thought that dovetail drawer joints are a sign of well manufactured, high quality furniture. Today this does not always hold true. Many products are made of composition board and paper products. It is quite possible to come across drawers with wooden fronts and cardboard sides with dovetails photographed on the wood grained cardboard. Some sides are cast from plastic with photographed dovetails. It is a good idea to check carefully before purchasing furniture.

The typical drawer construction can be one of two methods using dovetail joints. The first method involves cutting dovetails in the side and front edges with a dovetail jig. (See figure 8–B–1). The second method is a linear dovetail cut into the drawer front. (See figure 8–B–2). This method is often used on flush overlapping drawer fronts.

Figure 8–B–1 Dovetails are cut in the side and front of the drawer.

Figure 8–B–2 Linear dovetails are cut into a drawer front.

The sides may have a mold on top for decoration. (See figure 8–B–3). There is a dado near the bottom of the sides to receive the drawer bottom. Another dado at the back of the sides holds the drawer back in place.

Figure 8–B–3 Drawer sides may have molded tops.

A drawer is made up of five pieces. (See figures 8–B–4 and 8–B–5).

Figure 8–B–4 Linear dovetail drawer pieces.

Figure 8–B–5 Drawer pieces with sides and front dovetailed.

To assemble the drawer, slide the sides into the drawer front. (See figure 8–B–6). Slide the back into the back dados and nail it in place. (See figure 8–B–7). Slide the drawer bottom into the side bottom dados. (See figure 8–B–8). Turn the drawer over and square it up with a framing square. Place two nails through the bottom into the drawer back. The drawer is complete.

Some drawers have a dado in the drawer sides. (See figure 8–B–9). This provides a slot to receive a wooden drawer slide.
NOTE: Never use the same kind of wood for both the side and the slide. They have a tendency to wear one another out.

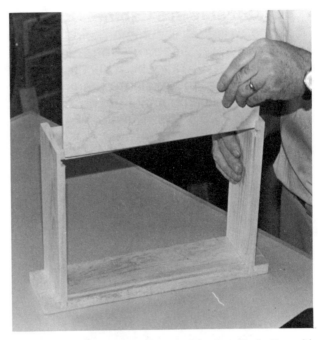

Figure 8–B–8 The drawer bottom slides into the bottom side dados.

Figure 8–B–6 The drawer sides fit onto the drawer front.

Figure 8–B–9 Side dados receive a wooden drawer slide.

Figure 8–B–7 The back fits into the back side dados.

C. Dovetail in a Cabinet Door

The dovetail is a common joint used to fasten drawers together. Sometimes the dovetail can be used for both decoration and fastening strength. A simple cabinet door illustrates this combination. (See figure 8–C–1).

Figure 8–C–1 A pine cabinet door with cedar wedges.

Individual pieces of pine are laid in place. A diagonally notched jig is clamped across each end of the pine layout. (See figure 8–C–2). With a dovetail bit and template guide mounted on the router, clean out the wedge shaped dado according to the jig pattern. (See figure 8–C–3).

Figure 8–C–2 Clamp a wedge shaped jig across the positioned pine boards.

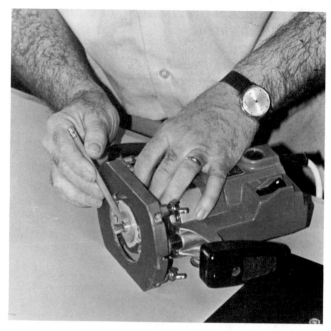

Figure 8–C–3 Use a template guide and a dovetail bit in the router to recess the pine in the jig pattern.

The depth of cut for these dados should not exceed one third the thickness of the pine material. The dado will have sloped sides. (See figure 8–C–4).

Figure 8–C–4 The recess will have sloped sides.

Using the same dovetail bit, joint a sloped edge on each side of the wedges cut to fit the dado. (See figure 8–C–5). These wedges may be made of a contrasting wood such as cedar. The wedges must be the thickness of the depth of cut of the pine material dados in order to fill the pattern cutout.

With both dados and wedges cut, assemble the door. The dovetail wedges slide into the dovetail dados fastening the pine pieces together. This makes a solid pine cabinet door with a decorative wedge shaped cedar strip. (See figure 8–C–6). They may be used as over lapping or flush mount doors.

Figure 8–C–5 Slope the sides of the wedges with the same dovetail bit.

Figure 8–C–6 Slide the wedges into the recesses fastening the pine pieces together to make a decorative cabinet door.

D. Surfacing

We often think the router can only be used for molds or fancy decorative cuts. It can also be used for smoothing uneven surfaces, such as log slices that are popular for table tops, clocks, and plaques. To surface the end of a log simply construct a wooden frame around the log and clamp it snugly in place. Make the frame as level or square as you choose to accomplish the surfacing desired. With an extended base and a flat bottom straight bit mounted in the router, set the desired depth of cut and slide the router back and forth across the frame until the entire surface has a smooth finish. (See figure 8-D-1). If the log is large this may take several passes. The relatively smooth finish should only require minimum sanding. If the log surface is extremely uneven, it may be necessary to reset the depth of cut and repeat the procedure several times.

To surface a larger log, such as the type used for table tops, the base plate on the router must be long enough to be in constant contact with two sides of the surrounding frame. (See figure 8-D-2). To speed up the process, more than one router may be mounted on the long base plate. One pass would then surface several areas of the log at one time.

NOTE: If more than one router is used, be sure all the routers are set at the same depth of cut.

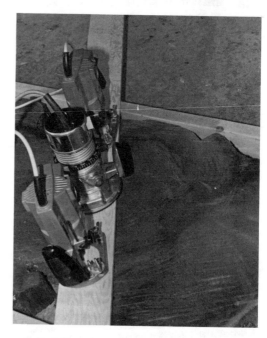

Figure 8-D-2 For a larger log surface use several routers on an extended base plate.

E. Provincial Door Design

There are many jigs on the market that you may purchase to put all sorts of designs on your cabinet doors or side panels. A very simple adjustable jig can be used to decorate your cabinet doors. (See figure 8-E-1). This jig has dovetail slots down the entire length. A dovetail pin is milled into each end of the cross pieces. The pieces simply slide together to form a square or rectangular jig which adjusts to any size cabinet door. Corner blocks of different designs can be used to change the square design. These corner blocks have dovetail pins milled into one side and one end. Simply slide them into place on the jig. (See figure 8-E-2).

Figure 8-D-1 Smooth a log end with the router.

Figure 8–E–1 Use a jig to decorate the face side of cabinet doors.

Figure 8–E–2 Change designs by using different corner blocks or make a square design by removing the corner blocks altogether.

Figure 8–E–3 The guide follows the jig pattern while the bit turns freely inside the guide.

Figure 8–E–4 Complete the decorative cut.

Figure 8–E–5 Remove the door from the jig.

Clamp the jig to the door. Mount a decorative plunge bit in the router. Fasten a template guide on the router base. The guide will follow the jig while the bit turns freely inside the guide. (See figure 8–E–3).

Carefully rout the chosen design in the face of the cabinet door. (See figure 8–E–4 and 8–E–5).

The changeable corner blocks and different bits will make an unlimited variety of door designs.

F. Raised Panel Doors

Construction of raised panel doors has always eluded the small shop woodworker, because of the lack of machinery and cutters. We now are seeing more and more combinations of router bits designed to make the panel door cuts. When purchasing a set of bits to make rails, stiles, and panels, be sure that it will do the job simply and accurately. I have not had much success with the type of stile and rail bits that are reversible. While milling the stiles, the face side is down against the router table. To cope the ends of the rails, the face side is up. This makes it difficult to get the face sides to come out flush. I have also noted a few raised panel bit sets on the market that are over 3" in diameter with a ¼" bit shank. I just don't feel there is enough strength in the small shank to hold that size cutter, particularily when it may be mounted in a light utility router. A cutter of this size should have a shank of ½" and be used in a router that is sized to run the cutter. It is not so much the small HP that bothers me but the physical size of the armature shaft, the bearings, and the chucks.

Each time I build a panel door, I think of the panel doors my father made with his Stanley #55 hand plane. This was an art in itself. The router has made the task much easier.

When constructing panel doors keep safety in mind. Always clamp where possible and use effective push sticks, hold downs, and special fences. I use a special table base plate and fences to accommodate these large bits. (See figure 8–F–1). The following will illustrate panel cutting with router bits to show cutters, the large hole plate, the use of set up blocks, safety hints, fences, hold downs, guards, and special mitre jigs together with sample door size calculations and gluing hints.

Figure 8–F–1 Use special fences and push sticks.

Panel Door Construction
Safety First

— Never run a cutter without a special fence and effective safety guards.

— Use push sticks and back-up blocks.

— Use a mitre jig and hold down clamp on all end grain cuts.

— When cutting cathedral top doors always mount the stock in jigs and use hold down clamps.

— If pilot cutting is necessary always guard the cutter, mount the stock in a jig with a hold down and use a safety guide pin.

Door Lip Cutter

Set the cutter to the desired height to make rounding over or bead to match the ⅜'' offset hinge. (See figure 8–F–2).

Figure 8–F–2 Molding with the door lip cutter.

Bead And Cope Cutters

Always cut the cope on the end of the rail first. This will allow for the bead cutter to clean any chipping. Raise the cutter so that the shoulder at A equals shoulder B. (See figure 8–F–4).

Glue Joint Cutter

This cutter is designed to handle a variety of thicknesses of stock. However, it must be set regardless of the thickness so that the pieces match when one is reversed. The cutter height from the router table must be exactly centre of the stock. (See figure 8–F–3).

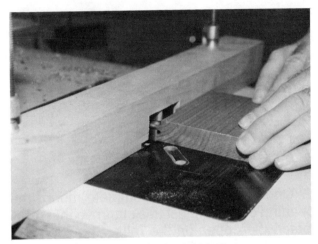

Figure 8–F–3 Molding with a glue joint cutter.

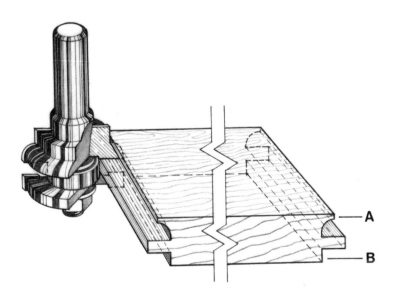

Figure 8–F–4 Cope cutter.

Be sure to use a fence and safe guards. Clamp the rail in a mitre jig with a backing block when cutting the cope in the ends of the rails. (See figure 8–F–5).

This pair of matched cutters are designed to always mill stile and rail parts face side down against your router table top. (See figure 8–F–7 and 8–F–8).

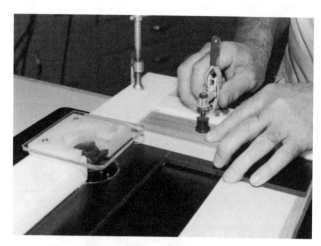

Figure 8–F–5 Cut the cope in the end of the rail.

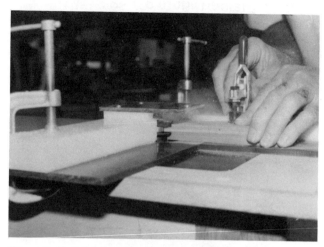

Figure 8–F–7 Cutting the rail face down on the table.

Once the copes are complete mount the beading cutter. Adjust this cutter so that it will match the copes on the rails. Shoulder A is equal to shoulder B. (See figure 8–F–6).

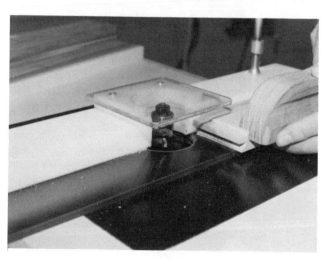

Figure 8–F–8 Cutting the stile face down on the table.

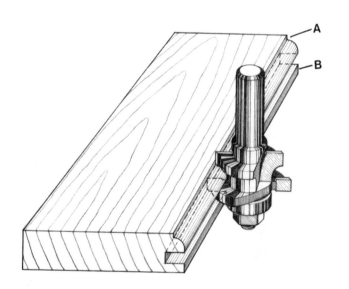

Figure 8–F–6 Bead cutter.

Raised Panel Cutter

Use a raised Panel Cutter for this operation. (See figure 8–F–9).

The recessed width must extend right to the pilot. Raise the cutter so that the flat tongue fits snugly into the dado on the stile and rail. (See figure 8–F–10, 8–F–11, and 8–F–12).

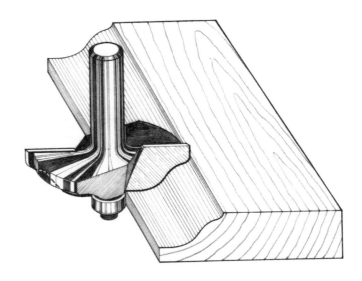

Figure 8–F–9 Panel cutter.

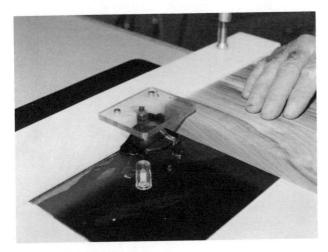

Figure 8–F–10 Cut the panel.

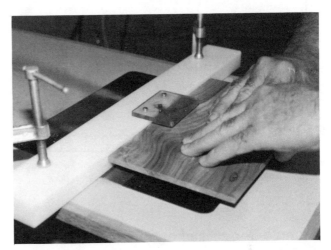

Figure 8–F–11 Tongue thickness must match groove in stile and rail.

Figure 8–F–12 All parts must fit together snugly.

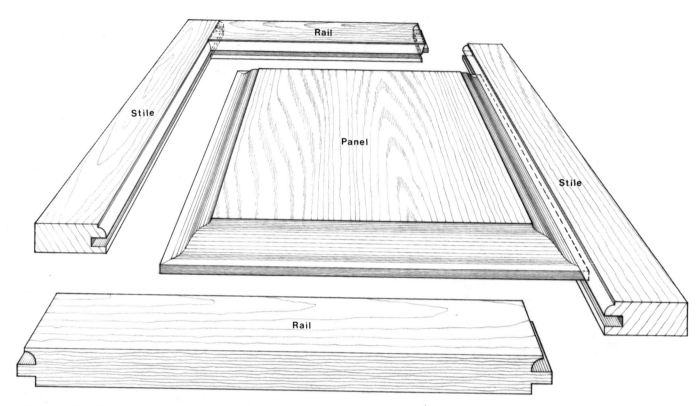

Figure 8–F–13 Exploded drawing of raised panel door.

Sample Door Size For Calculation Purposes

Plane the stiles and rails to ¾'' thickness.
Plane the panel to ⅝'' thickness.

Rails and stiles should be ripped and jointed to 2 and ⅜'' wide to give ample room for edge mold, rabbets, and hinge mounting. The bead and cope cutter will cut ⅜'' deep. Therefore, the following is a cut list needed for a sample door (12'' wide by 16'' long).

	wide	long	thick	
2	2 ⅜''	16''	¾''	stiles
2	2 ⅜''	8''	¾''	rails
1	8''	12''	⅝''	panel

(See figure 8–F–13, 8–F–14, and 8–F–15).

Gluing Hint

Never glue the panel in place. Let it float. Glue only the cope joint to the beaded rail. (See figure 8–F–16).

ALWAYS CHECK FOR SQUARE.

Figure 8–F–14 Raised panel door parts ready for assembly.

Figure 8–F–15 Raised panel door.

Figure 8–F–16 Glue only the rail to the stile.

119

OPEL

Marquetry by Allan E. Fitchett

Unit 9
Router Maintenance

Maintenance is the day by day attention to minor repairs to prevent major break downs. Major break down means down time for the equipment. In a school, router down time means a loss of class time that the students can never regain. In industry, the down time means a lack of production, which leads to financial loss. For the hobbyist, down time is discouraging.

Preventative maintenance done on a day to day basis can avert costly repairs and break downs as well as limit the amount of down time for the unit.

As with any piece of equipment, routers have parts that are most susceptible to wearing because of use. Should the router fail to start, first check the cord, the plug, and the switch. These parts take a certain amount of heavy duty use and therefore require maintenance. Cord damage usually occurs at the top of the router. This is due to the twisting and bending it receives during the use of the router. Faulty plugs and switches should be repaired without delay for safety reasons. (See figure 9–1).

When the router is running, check for excessive sparking at the top where the brushes are located. Excessive sparking could mean worn brushes. Be sure to unplug the router before removing the brushes. If they are worn to less than ¼" length, install new brushes. Worn brushes and excessive sparking can cause damage to the armature end where they contact. To ensure efficient operation this damage must be cleaned and smoothed. It is wise to have this properly machined. Never try to clean the armature with emery cloth or sandpaper.

If the brushes are not worn, perhaps the lead wire to the brush is disconnected. (See figure 9–2). Install a new brush. They are relatively inexpensive. This minor replacement could mean much in the way of trouble free performance.

Routers collect a great deal of dust and chips, particularily when they are table mounted. A regular cleaning of the work area and the router can reward the operator with more efficient and safe operation.

Figure 9–1 Faulty plugs are dangerous.

Figure 9–2 Check the lead wire to the brush for breakage.

Once the operator is accustomed to the router sound, any noticeable change in sound should be a call for maintenance inspection. Listen for grating, high-pitched whine, and rattles which may mean bad bearings. Continued use of a router with bad bearings leads to major and expensive repairs as well as lost time.

Figure 9–3 Router fan disintegrated.

Dull cutters cause most of the router damage that ever occurs. Dull bits and cutters set up terrific vibration because of the resistance between the cutter and the stock. This vibration can cause damage to bearings and/or cause disintegration of the fan. (See figure 9–3).

A relatively simple, periodic maintenance program that includes a check of power cords, plugs, switches, brushes, and bearings along with a policy of always using sharp cutters and bits can reward the router owner with long efficient service.

"A MACHINE WORTH USING IS WORTH THE PROPER CARE."

Care and Use of Carbide Bits And Cutters

Carbide bits and cutters provide economical and long lasting service with the proper care. They often last ten to twenty times as long as high speed steel bits. Carbide is a hard brittle material designed to withstand the force of normal cutting. Bumps, shocks, or vibrations can chip or crack the carbide. To obtain maximum efficiency from tungsten carbide bits and cutters, care and maintenance is essential.

As a sharp blow to the carbide could crack or shatter it, never drop or strike a carbide tipped tool.

All router bits should be mounted rigidly in the collet. Slippage or vibration causes an uneven cutting load which can damage the bit and the collet.

The router should be at full speed before starting the cut. A steady feed and uniform load create the ideal situation.

Do not cut into materials that contain nails, screws, etc. These obstructions will damage the cutter.

Check the cutters often. At the slightest sign of nicks or cracks, have the cutter serviced.

A poorly finished product or the need to increase feed pressure are indicators that the cutting edge is dull. Replace the cutter with a sharp clean one.

Carbide tools may need frequent cleaning and honing. Hand hones are available to remove accumulated wood dust and wood fluids. Use light smooth strokes and keep the hone clean.

If the cutting edge cannot be restored by honing because of nicks and cracks, have the tool reground by an experienced mechanic. Use a competent local grinding service. (See figure 9-4).

Storage of carbide tip bits and cutters is very important. Because of its brittle nature, carbide bits and cutters should be stored in individual wrappings. They may be stored in a special wooden bit box that has individually drilled shank holes in a wood block with lid protection (See figure 9-5). Some bits are stored in a sliding tray in the router bench. (See figure 9-6).

Figure 9-4 Special equipment and knowledge ensures expert router bit sharpening. This photo courtesy of Paul's Grinding Industries Ltd.

Figure 9-5 Carbide tipped bits and cutters must be stored individually to guard against chipping of the carbide.

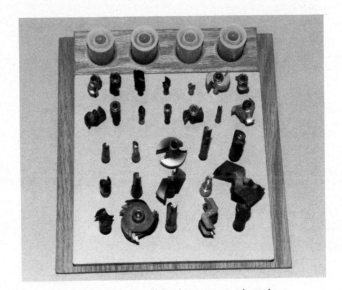

Figure 9-6 Tray storage slides into a router bench.

If wood was to be invented, it would be hailed as the greatest invention of all time. But when it comes to the manufacture of fine wood products it sometimes takes a little more than just a well chosen piece of wood.

When producing a fine crafted project, the router can make you look like a skilled craftsman. The router will cut those tight fitting joints, those fancy molded edges, those smooth bold lines, and those intricately carved designs that make one proud of the product. The following pictures are only a small collection of the many products that may be built with the help of the router. The list of products can be as long and varied as your imagination and creativity allow.

Figure 10–1 Table crafted by Luther Judt.

Figure 10–2 High back pine chair.

Figure 10–3 Tear drop table.

Figure 10–4 Everything from cheese blocks to picture frames can be made with a router.

Figure 10–5 Do pattern and circle work with a router.

Figure 10–6 Butterfly inlays strengthen joints and decorate the product.

Figure 10–7 Chess board crafted by Bob Swanson.

Figure 10–8 Trivet and cookie dish.

Figure 10–9 Walnut chest crafted by Jay Hatfield.

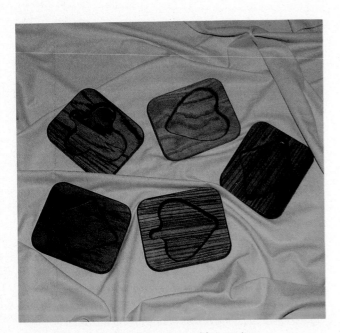

Figure 10–10 Candy dishes made with a router.

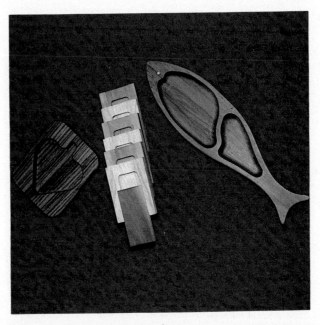

Figure 10–11 More pattern products.

Figure 10–12 A bank or kleenex box cover makes a nice gift.

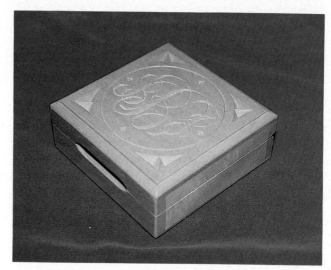

Figure 10–13 Box chip carved by Wayne Barton.

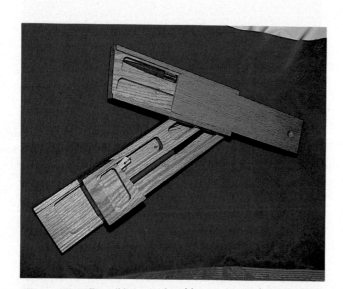

Figure 10–14 Pencil box made with a router and patterns.

Figure 10–15 Stacking boxes fit one inside the other.

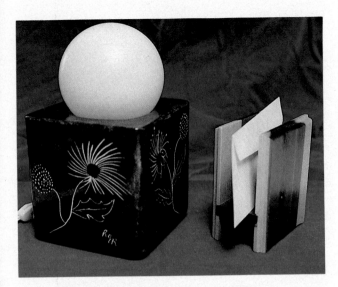

Figure 10–16 Rout a letter holder for your desk.

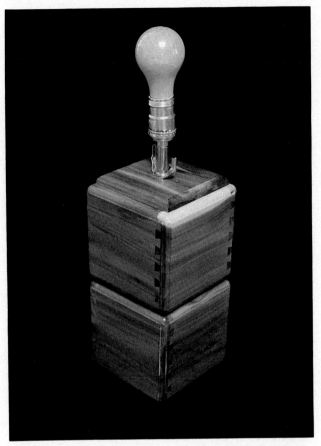

Figure 10–17 Dovetail corners and mold wood for a lamp.

Figure 10–18 Make pen stands and stamp boxes.

Figure 10–19 Circle work.

133

Figure 10–20 Rout oval mirror frames and wooden light fixtures.

Figure 10–21 Routed moldings make a beautiful square mirror frame.

134